THERE'S NO CREAM IN CREAM SODA

Facts and Folklore
About Our Favorite Drinks

Written by Kim Zachman
Illustrated by Peter Donnelly

RP|KIDS
PHILADELPHIA

Running Press Kids
Hachette Book Group
1290 Avenue of the Americas, New York, NY 10104
www.runningpress.com/rpkids
@RP_Kids

Printed in China

First Edition: July 2023

Published by Running Press Kids, an imprint of Perseus Books, LLC, a subsidiary of Hachette Book Group, Inc.
The Running Press Kids name and logo are trademarks of the Hachette Book Group.

The Hachette Speakers Bureau provides a wide range of authors for speaking events. To find out more,
go to www.hachettespeakersbureau.com or email HachetteSpeakers@hbgusa.com.

Running Press books may be purchased in bulk for business, educational, or promotional use.
For more information, please contact your local bookseller or the Hachette Book Group
Special Markets Department at Special.Markets@hbgusa.com.

The publisher is not responsible for websites (or their content)
that are not owned by the publisher.

Print book cover and interior design by Frances J. Soo Ping Chow.

Library of Congress Cataloging-in-Publication Data:
Names: Zachman, Kim, author. | Donnelly, Peter, 1967– illustrator.
Title: There's no cream in cream soda: facts and folklore about our favorite drinks / Kim Zachman;
illustrated by Peter Donnelly. Description: First edition. | Philadelphia: Running Press, [2023] |
Includes bibliographical references and index. | Audience: Ages 8–12 | Summary: "From soda to water to milk
and juice, There's No Cream in Cream Soda, the refreshing follow-up to There's No Ham in Hamburgers,
is full of fun facts and stories of the origins of some of America's most popular drinks"—Provided by publisher.
Identifiers: LCCN 2022025335 (print) | LCCN 2022025336 (ebook) | ISBN 9780762481323 (hardcover) |
ISBN 9780762481330 (ebook) Subjects: LCSH: Beverages—Juvenile literature. | Beverages—Miscellanea—
Juvenile literature. Classification: LCC TX815 .Z33 2023 (print) | LCC TX815 (ebook) |
DDC 641.87/5—dc23/eng/20220815 LC record available at https://lccn.loc.gov/2022025335
LC ebook record available at https://lccn.loc.gov/2022025336

ISBNs: 978-0-7624-8132-3 (hardcover), 978-0-7624-8133-0 (ebook)

APS

10   9   8   7   6   5   4   3   2   1

✳ Table of Contents ✳

Author's Note

When I started researching beverages, I was surprised at how many different kinds there are.

The team at Rocket Fizz Soda Pop and Candy Shop estimates that there are more than one thousand types of sodas in the United States and probably ten thousand in the world. There are so many brands of bottled waters that grocery stores have an entire aisle devoted to them. Stores also have long refrigerated cases full of dairy and plant-based milks. Don't even get me started on coffees. One coffee writer estimated that there are fifty-five thousand ways to order a drink at Starbucks.

When you consider that humans require only water to survive, it's incredible to think about how we keep creating more ways to hydrate. This thirst for new beverages has led to remarkable inventions, innovations, and discoveries.

For example, the need for safe water influenced the germ theory of disease. The desire for carbonated water inspired the discovery of carbon dioxide. And vitamin C was identified while studying why citrus fruit juices prevented scurvy.

Beverages have had an enormous cultural influence on America too. Drugstore soda fountains used to be the center of the social scene as people gathered to try new flavors of fizzy sodas. Then coffee shops, with their endless lists of lattes, cappuccinos, and macchiatos became the main meeting places.

Even our constitution has been changed because of beverages. The 1920 Prohibition Act made alcoholic drinks illegal. Prohibition lasted for only thirteen years, but that was long enough for soft drinks to become entrenched in the daily lives of most Americans.

I've been amazed at how drinks have influenced science, medicine, history, and culture, and vice versa. I think you'll be amazed too. Cheers!

Chapter One
WATER, WATER, EVERYWHERE . . .

WATER, WATER, EVERYWHERE, / NOR ANY DROP TO DRINK. SAMUEL Taylor Coleridge was so right when he wrote that in 1798. Of all the water on Earth, we can only use 1 percent of it! The rest is ocean water or frozen in the polar ice caps. Finding that 1 percent of freshwater has been, and will continue to be, one of the biggest challenges for the human species (other species too!).

A long time ago, people kept things simple by living beside rivers and lakes. That worked for small villages, but as cities grew bigger, it was harder for all the citizens to walk to the river with their buckets. They wanted a better way to get the water from where it was to where they wanted it to be.

In ancient Rome, they piped in water from faraway rivers with massive stone troughs called aqueducts. From 312 BCE until 226 CE, the master Roman builders constructed eleven aqueducts that crossed ravines, cut through mountains, and ran underground. Some of them were fifty miles long. That steady flow of water from the aqueducts dumped into big storage tanks. Then lead pipes carried the water from the tanks into homes, public drinking fountains, and bathhouses.

ROMAN BATHS

The public baths were large structures with many different rooms. Bathers could choose the *caldarium* (a hot, steamy pool), or the *tepidarium* (a warm pool), or work out in the *palaestra* (gym) and then cool off in the *frigidarium* (a cold pool). Built in 306 CE, the Baths of Diocletian complex in Rome was as big as a shopping mall and could hold three thousand people.

✳✳ Well? ✳✳

Rome supplied its citizens with fresh, clean water as a type of public service, but most cities didn't. In medieval times, citizens dug their own wells or hauled buckets from the river. People dumped their waste anywhere. They wouldn't think twice about throwing their poop in the same river where they got their drinking water. It was a germy way to live . . . and die.

Even though people couldn't see the tiny disease-causing bacteria lurking in their contaminated rivers, they knew they were taking chances when they chugged water. Instead, they drank beer, wine, and hard cider. Only the desperately dehydrated drank water.

Centuries later, when the Europeans colonized America, they still had the mindset that everyone was on their own to find water. In 1625, when the Dutch established New Amsterdam on the island of Manhattan, they discussed building public wells. But it didn't happen because no one wanted to pay for it. That decision cost them, BIG.

In 1664, British ships sailed into the harbor. The Dutch ran to their fort, closed the gates, and got ready for a drawn-out battle. Except they forgot one thing—there were no wells inside the fort. The Dutch knew they wouldn't last long without water, so they surrendered. Without hardly firing a cannon, the British captured the colony and promptly renamed it New York.

✳✳ A Bottle of Health ✳✳

Since ancient times, people believed that natural mineral springs had healing powers. In the 1700s and early 1800s, people flocked to these springs to "take the waters." Cities like Lourdes, France, and Bath, England, built a thriving tourism business out of catering to sickly people seeking cures. Americans were "taking the waters," too, in towns like Saratoga Springs,

New York (the birthplace of the potato chip), and Warm Springs, Georgia (President Franklin D. Roosevelt's favorite place to soak).

For a few extra dollars, guests could buy a bottle of healing spring water to take home with them. In Saratoga Springs, the Saratoga Mineral Water company began bottling spring water in 1820. Another early brand, Poland Spring, started in 1845 in Maine. After winning a Medal of Excellence at the Chicago World's Fair in 1893, it became the top brand in America.

SPRINGING OUT OF THE GROUND

When underground water flows out onto the surface of the earth, it's called a spring. Different geological factors determine if the spring is mineral, thermal, or sweet (no minerals at all). Some springs are naturally bubbly because carbon dioxide has dissolved in the water. The famous Perrier water from Vergèze, France, is an example of that. There are geothermal mineral springs all over the world, including 1,600 in the United States. People love to soak in these natural bathtubs with temperatures ranging from a warm 88 degrees Fahrenheit like Warm Springs in Georgia to hotter ones like Saratoga Hot Springs in Utah at 110 degrees. When water goes deep into the earth, it gets heated by the high temperatures near the core. Minerals dissolve into the water as it rises back to the surface. Some minerals are beneficial, such as lithium, zinc, and magnesium, but some are toxic, such as arsenic and sulfur. There are cold springs as well, with temperatures in the fifties—a bit chilly for bathing, but very refreshing to drink.

They weren't the only ones. Almost every mineral spring had a bottling company on its shore. They all claimed to cure a wide range of illnesses from constipation to cancer. They didn't, of course, but at least they were safe to drink, unlike the dangerously contaminated well water in crowded cities.

✳ The Disease Detective ✳

In the early 1800s, the medical community believed that miasma (poisonous air) caused illness. One London doctor, John Snow, didn't think it made sense that miasma could be the explanation for all diseases. Even though he didn't know about germs yet, he thought cholera "poisons" might be in the water instead of the air. He wrote a pamphlet about it in 1849, but no one took it seriously.

He got a chance to test his theory in August 1854 when a terrible cholera outbreak hit the Soho area of London. Five hundred people died in less than two weeks. He plotted the addresses of the victims on a large map and discovered that all but two people had been within a quarter mile of a public well known as the Broad Street Pump. He interviewed the other two victims' families and discovered that they had gotten water from that well too.

Snow convinced the mayor to take the handle off the pump so no one else could use it and the outbreak stopped. It was the first time anyone had tracked down the source of infection by studying where people lived. Snow's discovery led to a new field of medicine called epidemiology (the study of disease in populations). His map of death is known as the "Ghost Map."

Other scientists began to question the miasma theory, including French scientist Louis Pasteur, who did groundbreaking research in the late 1850s. Because of Pasteur's and other scientists' work, germ theory finally blew the miasma theory away.

CHOLERA

The bacterium *Vibrio cholerae* causes cholera. The symptoms include watery diarrhea, vomiting, and leg cramps. It can be fatal within a few hours if not treated. Italian physician Filippo Pacini discovered this bacterium in 1854, but his discovery didn't reach the medical world. German scientist Robert Koch rediscovered it in 1883. Although rare in the United States now, cholera still occurs frequently in parts of the world with poor sanitation. There are an estimated three million cases each year and eighty thousand to ninety-five thousand deaths.

Sneaky Treatment

Even though the medical community finally knew what caused cholera, they weren't sure what to do about it. New Jersey doctor John Leal had heard about a typhoid outbreak in England that had been stopped by adding chlorine to the water. When he started working for the Jersey City Water Supply Company in New Jersey in 1902, he decided to try to prevent outbreaks instead of waiting for them to happen. Without asking permission or telling anyone, he added chlorine to the Jersey City water system.

When people found out, they went berserk! They thought Leal had poisoned them! They sued him. However, when Leal showed the judge how his chlorine treatments reduced the number of bacteria in the water from thirty thousand per milliliter to the astoundingly low SIX per milliliter, the judge decided that chlorine was good and dropped the case.

Other American cities began chlorinating their water and, within decades, deaths from waterborne bacteria dropped by 95 percent.

✳✳ Flowing Fountains and Bubbling Bubblers ✳✳

For hundreds of years, people were afraid to drink water because they didn't know if it was safe. They drank other things instead, like tea, coffee, and beer. In the 1870s, the Women's Christian Temperance Union (WCTU) wanted to give people more opportunities to drink water. They worked with cities all over the United States to install public drinking fountains with fresh, clean water. The WCTU asked wealthy citizens to contribute to the cost. Donating fountains became a competition of generosity among the superrich. Not only did they give huge, elaborately designed structures, but they also had

formal ceremonies to mark the occasion. When the famous circus owner P. T. Barnum donated a fountain in his hometown of Bethel, Connecticut, in August 1881, the fire department, the police department, and a marching band paraded to the fountain and then Barnum gave a speech.

These fountains had much cleaner water, but they still weren't germ-free because of *how* people drank from them. Each fountain had a metal cup attached to it by a chain and everyone used it. Talk about catching cooties! It finally dawned on people that this wasn't hygienic, and a "Ban the Cup" campaign started. It took a while, but in 1909, Kansas outlawed communal cups. Other states followed soon after.

But people really liked the water fountains. How were they going to get a drink now? Lawrence Luellen solved that problem. He invented the disposable paper cup in 1907. He originally called it the Health Kup, but later changed it to Dixie Cup.

Luellen's disposable cup was a good idea, but Luther Haws had an even a better idea. How about a fountain that didn't need a cup? While serving as the sanitation inspector for the city of Berkeley, California, in 1906, Haws was at an elementary school when he watched with disgust as one kid after another drank from the same cup at the water fountain. Determined to come up with a better way, he invented the first drinking fountain that shot the water out in an arc. No cup needed at all! Soon every school, office building, and hospital had drinking fountains.

✳✳ Back to Bottles We Go ✳✳

Between safer tap water and sanitary fountains, Americans didn't need expensive bottled water anymore, so business dried up. But not forever, because new dangers lurked.

For decades, industries and manufacturers dumped their waste into rivers and lakes, and these toxic chemicals seeped into the city water systems. Just like in the seventeenth and eighteenth centuries, people were contaminating their own water sources again, but this time with poisonous chemicals.

In 1969, the Cuyahoga River in Cleveland was so polluted by industrial chemicals, it actually caught fire! The burning river got the attention of environmentalists, and they pushed for and finally succeeded in getting the Clean Water Act passed in 1972 and the Safe Drinking Water Act in 1974.

These new laws helped clean things up a lot. However, another poison lurked in our water, and it came from the pipes themselves!

LEAD

Lead is the eighty-second element on the periodic table and is represented as Ph from the Latin word for lead, *plumbum.* Our word "plumber" means someone who works with lead. Lead is rarely found in its pure form, but instead is usually found in ores that are mined in the western United States. Exposure to it can cause permanent brain damage, especially in children. Before we knew that lead was toxic, it was used in cosmetics, paint, pipes, and gasoline.

Water pipes had been made of lead since the Roman times. Lead doesn't rust, it's easy to bend and shape, and it doesn't decay when buried underground. So, when cities installed water pipes in the late 1800s and early 1900s, lead seemed like the perfect choice. They didn't know then what we know now.

Research in the 1940s showed a definite link between high levels of lead in the blood and brain damage in children, but it wasn't until the late 1970s that public concern reached a point where the Environmental Protection Agency (EPA) began widespread testing of city water supplies. Where there were high levels of lead, the pipes were treated with special coatings to keep it from leaching into the water. Unfortunately, those coatings didn't always work, a failure that continues to impact communities around the country, including Flint, Michigan, in 2014.

The public's trust in tap water took another dip in 1986 after EPA employees began testing school water fountains. They found shockingly high levels of lead in the water because the fountains had lead parts. The fountain makers had to scramble to redesign their products and replace them.

The bottled water industry took advantage of the public's distrust. In 1977, Europe's best-selling mineral water, Perrier, launched a five-million-dollar ad campaign to convince Americans that Perrier's naturally carbonated mineral spring water was worth paying for. Other water bottlers ramped up their marketing campaigns as well. The underlying message of the bottled water companies' advertising was that their water was safer and cleaner and tasted better than tap water.

Another boon for bottled water was the development of PET plastic bottles in the 1970s. These cheap, convenient, lightweight bottles completely changed the drinking habits of Americans. The sales of bottled water went from approximately 350 million gallons in the 1970s to 15 BILLION gallons in 2020. We now buy more bottled water than any other beverage, and those bottles are filling up our landfills.

PET BOTTLES

In 1973, Nathaniel Wyeth patented a new bottle made of polyethylene terephthalate (PET). Lighter and cheaper than glass, PET bottles were immediately adopted by the soft drink industry and, not long after, the bottled water companies. Although PET bottles are easily recyclable, only approximately 30 percent gets recycled in the United States. According to the Ocean Conservancy's annual beach cleanups, plastic bottles are the third most collected trash. These plastic bottles might be littering our bodies too. When analyzed, 93 percent of bottled waters were found to contain microplastics. Research has only recently begun to determine the health consequences of microplastics, but early studies have shown that they may interfere with normal hormone functions.

But the competition for consumer dollars is stiff and companies are always looking for ways to attract buyers' attention. To make their products stand out on the grocery store shelves, manufacturers offer sparkling, mineral, purified, fortified, enhanced, and flavored waters. Sometimes they claim extra health benefits of their waters, just like the early bottlers of the mineral springs did hundreds of years ago. Whether they're healthier than plain old tap water is a matter of debate, but they're certainly more interesting.

OH NO! NUTRITION

There's a common saying that we should drink eight glasses of water a day. But that's not enough for a three-hundred-pound football player practicing on a hot day. And it's too much for a newborn. The amount of water needed depends on body weight, activity level, and diet. It also matters how much water-packed fruits and vegetables are being eaten. Other beverages contribute to hydration too. So, how do you know if you are getting enough water? If you're thirsty, you're not.

TOP IT OFF

- Astronauts on the International Space Station have been drinking their urine since 2009. Water from urine, sweat, and the air is captured, purified, and used again.
- The kangaroo rat of North America can go its entire lifetime (about ten years) without water. It has adapted in several ways to help conserve fluids, including specialized kidneys that filter urine to keep water in the body.
- A 750-milliliter bottle of Svalbardi Polar Iceberg Water costs around $100. It's harvested from four-thousand-year-old Arctic icebergs.
- The Grand Prismatic Spring in Yellowstone National Park is the third largest spring in the world at 370 feet in diameter and one of the hottest at 160 degrees Fahrenheit.

✳✳ Concoction Corner ✳✳

In 1979, on a live radio show in Los Angeles, California, Bruce Nevins, the president of Perrier, was given seven unmarked cups of sparkling waters, one of which was Perrier. He was challenged to identify his brand by taste alone. He failed four times before finally guessing the right one.

Some people say they drink a certain brand of bottled water because it tastes good. But can they really tell a difference? Let's test the tasters.

WATER TASTE TEST

YOU'LL NEED:

- 25 (4-ounce) cups
- 4 different brands of non-sparkling bottled water in at least 16-ounce bottles
- 20 ounces tap water
- 5 score sheets and pens
- 5 volunteer tasters

On a table, set five cups in a row. Pour a sample of each kind of water, including the tap water, into a cup. Be sure to track which kind of water goes into which cup. Bring one volunteer into the room at a time. Have them taste the water in each cup and mark whether they think it's bottled or tap and score it for taste. After all the volunteers have taken a turn, bring them back in together and reveal the brands.

How many did they get right? Did they agree? How often did tap water get a high score for taste?

SCORE SHEET EXAMPLE

Sample	Tap	Bottled	Taste 1–5 (5 = best)
#1			
#2			
#3			
#4			
#5			

Chapter Two

MILK IT FOR ALL IT'S WORTH

HUMANS HAVE BEEN DRINKING MILK EVER SINCE THERE HAVE been humans. We're mammals after all, and all mammal babies start out with milk. But unlike other mammals, we drink all different kinds.

Archaeologists believe that sheep, goats, and cows were the first animals to be domesticated around ten thousand years ago during the Neolithic period. Historians aren't sure when milking caught on, but it's safe to say it didn't happen right away. It probably took a few generations of taming the animals before they would stand quietly while someone tugged on their udder.

That would have been especially true of cows. Modern cattle are descended from the mighty aurochs. Those giant, fiercely aggressive animals stood six feet tall at the shoulder and had long curved horns for impaling predators. Walking into a tiger's den would've been safer than trying to milk an auroch.

But humans are persistent creatures, and, eventually, we got the sweet-faced bovine that we know and love today. Although goats and sheep were milked, too, cows have become the dairy divas for a simple reason—they make the most milk. A typical goat might produce one and a half gallons a day and a sheep even less. When you compare that to the average dairy cow that squirts out an astounding seven to eight gallons a day, there's no contest.

Fresh milk spoils so quickly that humans didn't use much dairy in the beginning. That all changed about eight thousand years ago when some bacteria fell into a bowl of milk and—ta-da!—yogurt happened. That yummy, creamy stuff was an excellent addition to humans' daily diet. After that discovery, milk mattered . . . a lot! This became triply true when people figured out how to make cheese and butter around six thousand years ago.

NEOLITHIC PERIOD (10,000-3,000 BCE)

The Neolithic period marked the beginning of human civilization as people evolved from small groups of hunters and gatherers into permanent farming communities. The earliest evidence of farming dates to about twelve thousand years ago in the Fertile Crescent, an area in the Middle East that includes modern-day Iraq, Syria, Lebanon, Israel, Jordan, and Egypt. Fig trees and wheat were probably the first cultivated plants.

Moos to America

Throughout the Middle Ages, dairy products became a dietary staple for many civilizations. When Europeans began to colonize the Americas, they brought their cows with them because there were no cattle on the American continent.

As American cities grew, getting fresh milk became a challenge. Occasionally farmers led their cow into the city and milked it directly into their customers' jugs. Can't get much fresher than that! Some city dwellers kept a cow tied up in front of their house and would take it to a city park to graze. Instead of dog parks, they had cow parks.

However, not everyone could have their own personal cow, especially in crowded city neighborhoods. Urban dairies began to pop up in the 1820s to satisfy the demand. Unfortunately, these dairies were often built next to beer breweries. The poor cows were crammed into barns next to the brewery and then, instead of being fed hay and grains, they were fed the swill left over from making beer.

A combination of a poor diet and terrible living conditions resulted in sick cows producing thin, blue-tinted milk. The dairy workers knew the public wouldn't like it that way, so they added chalk to make it thicker and whiter.

Besides being poor quality, the swill milk was also full of germs. The cows lived in absolute filth and the milkmen didn't bother washing the buckets or their hands. Some cows had tuberculosis, which passed through their milk and infected whoever drank it.

TUBERCULOSIS FIGHTER ROBERT KOCH (1843-1910)

Tuberculosis is a contagious bacterial disease that typically attacks the lungs and can be fatal. In humans, the bacterium *Mycobacterium tuberculosis* is spread through coughing. In cows, the bacterium *Mycobacterium bovis* spreads to people through the infected cow's milk. The German scientist Robert Koch identified the tuberculosis bacterium in 1882. He also developed a diagnostic test that allowed farmers to identify infected cows and isolate them before they spread the disease to the rest of the herd. Koch was awarded the Nobel Prize for his work in 1905.

Milk Hero #1

Robert M. Hartley, the founder of the New York Temperance Society in 1829, believed alcohol was the root of all evil. He wanted to shut all the beer breweries down. While investigating breweries, he discovered the disgusting dairy barns. In 1842, he wrote a book called *An Historical, Scientific, and Practical Essay on Milk, as an Article of Human Sustenance* in which he described the horrible conditions at the barns. Hartley thought the swill milk might be the reason so many people were getting sick and dying. But no one believed him because they didn't know about germs yet.

The brewery barns kept selling swill milk, but Hartley didn't give up. Finally, *Frank Leslie's Illustrated Newspaper* listened to Hartley and published a scathing report about the dairies in 1858. The public got angry and demanded change. In 1862, New York State passed the Act to Prevent the Adulteration and Traffic of Impure Milk. After forty years of trying, Hartley's efforts paid off and the dirty dairies closed. For his hard work and dedication to saving lives, he's considered America's first consumer protector.

LOUIS PASTEUR (1822-1895)

Although best known for pasteurization, a heat-treatment process for eliminating bacteria from beverages, Louis Pasteur was one of the most important scientists in microbiology and chemistry of his era. He proved that germs existed and that they caused illness, which led to the germ theory of disease, effectively canceling the miasma theory. After inventing pasteurization, he did important work with vaccines, including developing vaccines for anthrax and rabies.

Meanwhile, over in France in 1865, Louis Pasteur was trying to figure out why some wines soured and others didn't. He believed microscopic organisms were causing the spoilage. To help his winery clients, Pasteur developed a method of heating the wine just hot enough and long enough to kill the offending bacteria, but not too hot or too long to ruin the wine. That method is known as pasteurization.

It wasn't until 1886 that Franz von Soxhlet, a German agricultural chemist, suggested the pasteurization process should be used on milk. Although some dairy farmers thought it was a great idea, others believed the heat destroyed the nutrients as well as the germs. Some people didn't like how it tasted.

Milk Hero #2

German immigrant Nathan Straus, co-owner of Macy's Department Stores in New York City, was convinced that pasteurization would save lives. Straus had a personal vendetta against contaminated milk because he believed it killed two of his children.

In 1893, with his own money, he built a pasteurization and bottling plant and then opened eighteen milk depots in low-income neighborhoods. He sold his milk for four cents a quart to those who could afford it and gave it away for free to those who couldn't. He also wrote pamphlets and gave public lectures about the benefits of pasteurization.

Unfortunately, there was still a lot of controversy. The big milk debate got the attention of President Theodore Roosevelt. He directed the Public Health Service to study it. They issued a report in 1908 that said pasteurization didn't damage the nutrients in milk or change its taste and that it was much safer than raw milk. That convinced a lot of people. That same year, Chicago became the first city to mandate the pasteurization of milk. By 1917, forty-six major US cities required it.

Now that milk was finally safe, Americans started drinking it by the gallons.

✳✳ Milk Hero #3 ✳✳

A scary thing happened on Gail Borden's voyage back to America from England in 1851. The ship's cows got sick and quit producing milk. They were kept on board to provide fresh milk for infants and children, and when they couldn't make milk, some of the babies almost starved to death. This near tragedy inspired Borden to find a better way to take milk on long journeys.

Borden developed a technique of heating the cream slowly at a low temperature in a vacuum pan until the water evaporated. The condensed milk could then be sealed in cans to prevent spoiling. Borden's Eagle Brand Sweetened Condensed Milk came out in 1856, and for the first time, milk didn't need refrigeration. No more seasick cows!

✳✳ Milk Hero #4 ✳✳

This sounds unbelievable to us today, but in the 1800s, milk was kept in open barrels where dust, leaves, sticks, and bugs fell into it. Street vendors carried open buckets of milk hung on a yoke that balanced on their shoulders.

In 1884, Dr. Henry G. Thatcher of Potsdam, New York, was standing in line to buy milk when a little girl in front of him accidentally dropped her dirty doll into the vendor's bucket. Acting like it was no big deal, the vendor scooped out the doll with his bare hands, handed it to the girl, and then filled her jug. Absolutely disgusted, Dr. Thatcher went home and created the Milk Protector, a sealable bottle that became the standard container for milk for years—at least until the inexpensive, disposable paper cartons took over in the 1940s.

FROM DOOR TO STORE

For many years, dairy farms delivered milk directly to customers' doors. The milkman would leave a quart or two of milk on the front porch and take away the empties. Then in 1915, John Van Wormer invented the paperboard milk carton. Not only did the cartons fit in refrigerators better, but they also didn't break. It took a while for the shoppers to come around to the new way of buying milk, but, eventually, they realized it was more convenient and cheaper to pick up a carton from the grocery store than pay for home delivery. By the 1950s, most milkmen were out of a job.

Homogenization

At the 1900 World's Fair in Paris, Auguste Gaulin introduced his *lait homogenisé* (milk homogenizer) machine. His device blended the milk so it wouldn't have globs of fat floating on the top. To the general public, this invention was a total yawner. But ice cream manufacturers were thrilled with it because it made their ice cream even creamier.

The dairies wanted to use it for milk, too, but their customers weren't interested. In 1932, the McDonald Dairy Company in Flint, Michigan, came up with the regurgitation comparison test to demonstrate the advantage of homogenized milk.

One group of test subjects drank regular milk and the other drank homogenized. Then they threw up into clear glass jars. The plain milk had curdled in the stomach while the homogenized milk stayed smooth. McDonald Dairy salesmen carried around the vomit jars to prove to people that they should buy homogenized milk. Although some people might have sworn off milk forever after seeing those jars, homogenized became the standard within a few years.

Shaking It Up

Since the 1890s, milkshakes had been popular at soda fountains and ice cream parlors. These desserts got their name because they were literally shaken in a covered container until the milk and ice cream blended into a smooth, creamy drink. Soda fountain servers got a serious workout making shakes.

The process got a whole lot easier in 1922 when Stephen Poplawski invented the blender. Although it saved the servers from sweating, it was still slow because it made only one shake at a time. In 1936, Earl Prince solved that problem with his Multimixer, a blender that could make several shakes at once.

In 1954, a Multimixer salesman named Ray Kroc heard about a burger joint in California with eight Multimixers. He wanted to know why they needed so many. He visited the McDonald brothers, Maurice (Mac) and Richard (Dick), at their restaurant. Kroc was blown away to learn that the McDonald brothers sold twenty thousand shakes a month. He was so impressed with their fast-food operation that he bought it. With nearly forty thousand stores in more than one hundred countries, McDonald's is the largest restaurant chain in the world, and it all started with milkshakes.

LACTOSE INTOLERANCE

Mother Nature came up with a brilliant plan so young mammals wouldn't keep pestering their moms for milk. She made sure that as soon as baby animals could eat solid foods, they wouldn't need milk anymore. Milk contains the sugar lactose, which is broken down by the enzyme lactase. Mammal babies have lactase, but they're genetically coded to quit making it after their teeth grow in. Without lactase, they can't digest milk, causing bloated intestines and diarrhea. This is true of humans as well. But about eight thousand years ago, that lactase gene mutated in people in Northern Europe and their lactase kept flowing. The mutated gene passed down through the generations, creating a population of lifelong milk drinkers. In some parts of the world, almost 100 percent of the population is lactose intolerant. However, in the United States, most people (60 to 65 percent) can still digest milk because they have European ancestors.

✳✳ The Not-Milk Milks ✳✳

Plant-based drinks that are commonly referred to as "milks" have been gaining in popularity in the last few years. Using almonds, oats, soy, coconuts, peas, or rice, these beverages are made by soaking the plant in water and then squeezing (or milking) out the liquid.

While they may seem like new products, almond milk and soy milk have been around for centuries. As long ago as the thirteenth century, European Christians had strict fasting rules, and dairy products were banned on certain days. They used almond milk instead. At about the same time, a soy-based drink became common in China.

Although the milk industry objects to the plant-based beverages using the word "milk," the public doesn't seem to care what they're called. Between the lactose-intolerant folk and the growing vegan movement, sales of these alternate milks have risen steadily year after year. Meanwhile, the sale of real milk has been in a slow decline. But like our Neolithic ancestors, we still love our yogurt and cheese.

OH NO! NUTRITION

Milk is an important source of protein, calcium, riboflavin, phosphorous, potassium, vitamins A and D, and niacin. The 2020–2025 Dietary Guidelines for Americans recommends three cups of dairy a day after age two. However, milk from cows can be high in saturated fats, so low-fat or nonfat milk, yogurts, and cheeses are recommended.

As for the plant-based milk alternatives, the closest in nutritional value is fortified soy milk. The other plant-based beverages aren't included in the milk category because they lack some of the important nutrients.

TOP IT OFF

- A hooded seal produces milk that is 60 percent fat. The seal pup drinks as much as sixteen pounds of milk a day. By the time they're weaned, in an amazingly short time of three to five days, they've almost doubled in size.
- In 1993, the California Milk Processor Board launched the "Got Milk?" advertising campaign. It's considered one of the most successful ads in history, with 90 percent of people in America aware of it.
- On October 5, 1818, Nancy Hanks Lincoln (Abraham Lincoln's mother) died of milk sickness because she drank poisoned milk from a cow that had eaten the toxic white snakeroot plant.
- Nakazawa Milk from Japan is the most expensive milk in the world. It comes from cows that are only milked once a week in the morning because that is when melatonin levels are the highest. Melatonin is believed to lower anxiety. Advertised as milk for stressed-out adults, one gallon of Nakazawa Milk costs the same as forty gallons of regular 2 percent milk, around $163 per gallon.

✳✦ Concoction Corner ✦✳

This super-easy experiment demonstrates molecular polarities with an amazing burst of color.

MILKY COLOR BLAST

YOU'LL NEED:

- 2 percent milk or whole milk
- Shallow plate
- 4 water-based food colorings
- Dish soap
- Cotton swab

Pour the milk into the dish so it's at least ¼ inch deep. Add one drop of each food coloring in the middle of the dish as close to one another as possible. Put a drop of dish soap on the end of the cotton swab and put it in the middle of the milk and hold it there for ten seconds.

Watch the colors swarm and swirl!

WHY THIS HAPPENS

Milk is mainly water, which is a polar molecule. Milk also contains fat molecules, which are nonpolar. The dish soap molecule has a nonpolar portion and a polar portion. The polar portion of the soap binds with the polar water molecule while the soap's nonpolar portion desperately wants to bind with the nonpolar fat molecule. As the nonpolar part of the soap moves through the milk to catch the fat molecules, it pushes the food colorings out of its way.

Chapter Three

ALL THE TEA IN CHINA

CAMELLIA *SINENSIS* ISN'T THE MOST IMPRESSIVE BUSH IN THE jungle. Its dense mass of green leaves and occasional small white blossoms wouldn't win any horticulture beauty contests. And yet, it's one of the most important plants on the planet because it makes the world's favorite beverage—tea.

According to Chinese mythology, the fabled finder of the fantastic leaf was the great emperor Shen-Nung. Around 2450 BCE, Shen-Nung was boiling water in a pot when he fell asleep under a tree. While he snoozed, leaves dropped into the pot. When he woke up, he discovered his water had turned into tea.

This wasn't Shen-Nung's only discovery. He's known as the Father of Chinese Medicine for finding 365 medical treatments made from plants. He also invented the plow and taught people how to grow crops, so his other title is Divine Farmer.

HOW TEA IS MADE

All teas come from a tea bush, *Camellia sinensis*, but it's *how* the leaves are processed that determines the type of tea. First, the leaves are spread in the sun to dry, which is known as withering. Leaves that are going to be black or oolong teas are then cut or crushed to help oxidation. During the oxidation phase, the leaves are exposed to air, which turns them darker and strengthens the flavor. Black teas are fully oxidized, oolong teas are partially oxidized, while green teas aren't oxidized at all. To keep green teas from oxidizing, they are gently heated or steamed instead. All leaves then go through rolling, shaping, and dehydrating.

The earliest archaeological evidence of tea is from the Zhou dynasty (around 1046–256 BCE). Historians believe the first tea drinkers were Buddhist monks who needed the caffeine to keep them awake during long meditations. As they traveled around China teaching and preaching Buddhism, they also spread the joy of tea.

China's population exploded during the Han dynasty (206 BCE–220 CE) to fifty million people, and that's partly because tea helped them stay healthy and alive. When the Chinese boiled water to make tea, it destroyed the bacteria that caused diseases such as cholera and diphtheria. During this time of health and prosperity, they invented paper, porcelain, gunpowder, and the compass.

Tea really took off after Lu Yu wrote *The Classic of Tea* in 761 CE. According to Lu Yu, brewing the perfect cup of tea required attention to

detail. His instructions included everything from when to pluck the leaves (never when it's raining) to how long to heat the tea cake (until it's pliable like a baby's plump arm). He also said that you should never get water from whirlpools, or the tea would give you a sore neck.

Being supremely picky like Lu Yu became a sign of refinement. If families could afford it, they hired professional tea masters. They also wanted something classy to drink it in. Chinese porcelain makers started producing thin, beautiful bowls for sipping perfectly brewed tea.

Traders coming into China on the great Silk Road found out about tea and they took it back to their countries. As if the poor camels didn't have enough to carry already, bricks of dried tea were added to their loads.

THE SILK ROAD IS NOT A ROAD

The Silk Road was a network of trade routes connecting Asia with the Middle East and Europe that was developed starting in 130 BCE. Although named for China's main export, porcelain, paper, tea, jade, and spices were also traded. Depending on the point of departure and the destination, traders could be on the road for over a year. Marco Polo traveled the Silk Road. He left Italy in 1272 and finally arrived in Xanadu, China, in 1275.

An English Cuppa

In 1610, Dutch traders brought tea back to Europe after visiting China. From the Dutch, tea slowly infused into the rest of Europe, reaching France in the 1630s and England in the 1650s. The English didn't get that excited about tea until 1662, when King Charles II married Princess Catherine of Portugal. She was an avid tea drinker, and her royal influence made it fashionable in high society.

HANDLE IT

Many Asian cultures believe that if a teacup is too hot to hold, the tea is too hot to drink. They use small bowls instead of cups. But the Brits liked their tea much hotter than the Chinese, so English potters began adding handles to their cups in the late 1700s.

Tea, coffee, and chocolate came to Europe at about the same time in the mid-1600s. No one had ever had caffeine before, so there was a lot of buzz about these new beverages. At first, English men preferred coffee, and they hung out in coffeehouses, discussing the issues of the day. Respectable ladies wouldn't dream of entering these "men dens," but they wanted to socialize too. In 1717, Thomas Twining opened the very first tea shop in London, giving women a place of their own. Tea shops popped up in many cities, towns, and villages.

Afternoon teas became important social events that gave families a chance to show off their fancy tea sets. After years of importing fine china from China, Josiah Wedgwood opened his pottery shop in 1759 so the English could finally buy local. Because of tea, England had a whole new porcelain industry.

✳✳ The Boston Tea Party ✳✳

A lot of American colonists had come from England or the Netherlands, both of which were tea-consuming countries. At first American colonists drank tea, too, but then the Revolutionary War happened.

It started when Britain and France had a battle over American territories known as the French and Indian War. Britain finally won in 1763, but wars are expensive, and they had a lot of bills to pay. The British Parliament decided that the American colonists should help cover the cost of the war. The Americans did not agree.

Parliament enacted the Townshend Acts in 1767, which taxed items such as paint, glass, paper, and tea. The colonists threw a fit. Parliament canceled all the taxes except the tea tax. The colonists responded by boycotting tea. Instead, they drank "Liberty Tea" made from roots, leaves, and berries of local plants, or they switched to coffee.

To appease the colonists but still get some tax money, Parliament passed the Tea Act in May 1773. This cut the cost of tea in half, but it still had a small tax on it. The Brits thought the colonists would be overjoyed at getting tea so cheaply and wouldn't mind that eensy-weensy tax. They were wrong. The colonists felt that it wasn't fair to pay taxes to a government that they had no say in. As Boston lawyer James Otis Jr. argued, "Taxation without representation is tyranny."

Tensions finally boiled over on December 16, 1773. Three British ships with 342 chests of tea had arrived in Boston Harbor. The colonists demanded that the Massachusetts governor, Thomas Hutchinson (a British loyalist), order the ships back to England. Nearly seven thousand people gathered at the Boston Meeting House waiting to hear the governor's answer. He said no. That's when the party got started.

A group of men, dressed like Mohawk people, boarded the ships and dumped the tea into the harbor. A crowd on the docks cheered them on. Things between the Brits and the colonists went downhill quickly after that, and on April 19, 1775, the Revolutionary War officially began at the Battle of Lexington.

Before the war, Americans had to buy tea from British companies. But after the war, they were free to buy directly from China. Robert Morris, a Philadelphia merchant and one of the signers of the Declaration of Independence, got some investors to pitch in, and they bought a ship, the *Empress of China*. It sailed out of New York on February 22, 1784, and came back fifteen months later filled to the brim with tea.

A year and a half is a long time for tea to be at sea. Sometimes it spoiled before reaching port. Beginning in the 1830s, American and Scottish shipbuilders tried to solve that problem by building faster ships. The "tea clippers" were smaller and lighter and had more sails.

The fastest ships earned top dollar for their tea, so it became a competition. Newspapers announced updates and people placed bets on their favorites like it was a horse race. One of the superstar ships, the American *Sea Witch,* left Canton, China, on January 8, 1849, and arrived in New York on March 25, setting a new record of seventy-nine days, less than half the time of a normal cargo ship.

The beautiful tea clippers became obsolete when the Suez Canal opened in 1869. Ships no longer had to sail around the tip of Africa, reducing the voyage by five thousand miles. The new steamships could make the trip in around fifty days.

THE GREAT TEA RACE OF 1866

On May 29, 1866, four ships loaded with tea left China and sailed to England. The first ship to dock in London would win a prize worth $50,000 in today's dollars. The *Fiery Cross* was the first clipper to leave the Chinese port of Fuzhou, with the *Ariel, Taeping,* and *Serica* following fourteen hours later. After sailing over fifteen thousand miles in ninety-nine days, the *Ariel* and *Taeping* entered the channel only ten minutes apart. The *Taeping* had a better tugboat and docked first to win the prize. The *Serica* came in one hour and fifteen minutes later for third place, and the poor *Fiery Cross* didn't make it until the next day.

Tea the American Way

After the Revolutionary War, Americans started drinking tea again, but not with the same gusto. They'd gotten used to coffee and never entirely switched back. Then Americans started doing something that was inconceivable to the rest of the tea-drinking world—they put ice in it.

Sweetened iced tea served with lemon became especially popular in the sweltering South. One often-told story claims that iced tea was introduced at the 1904 St. Louis World's Fair. While it's true that iced tea was sold at the fair, it wasn't new. The term "iced tea" is mentioned in newspapers dating as far back as the 1850s. The popularity of iced tea has never faltered. According to the Tea Association of the U.S.A., Inc., 75 to 80 percent of tea in America is served iced.

Lipton Tea, Please

Before Sir Thomas Lipton got involved with tea, he was a successful owner of a chain of grocery stores in Scotland. He didn't like paying the high prices charged by tea suppliers, so in 1890, he bought his own tea plantation in Sri Lanka (formally known as Ceylon). With his own supply, he could sell tea at a lower price than the competition.

Lipton also devised new packages for his tea in one-pound, half-pound, or quarter-pound sizes. Other grocery stores kept their tea leaves in big barrels. When a customer wanted some, the grocer scooped it out and wrapped it in paper. It was much easier for customers to grab a bag off the shelf than wait for the grocer to serve them. Lipton's prepackaged tea became a bestseller. In 1893, he opened the Thomas J. Lipton Company, in Hoboken, New Jersey. Americans loved Lipton Tea just as much as the English and Scottish did.

Lipton was the first to prepackage tea but not the first to put it in single-serving bags. The leading story about the invention of the tea bag credits Thomas Sullivan, a New York tea merchant. In 1908, Sullivan gave out samples of his tea in little silk pouches. Instead of opening the pouches, his customers put them directly in boiling water. It worked so well, they asked for more.

However, what Sullivan achieved by accident had already been invented in 1901 by Roberta Lawson and Mary McLaren from Milwaukee, Wisconsin. Their patent for a "tea leaf holder" was essentially the same thing except made with cotton fabric. Americans really liked the convenient bags, and by the 1930s, they were more common than loose tea. In 1952, the Lipton Company introduced its patented "flo-thru" four-sided tea bag that worked even better.

A New Tea Treat

Who would've thought dropping sweet, chewy tapioca balls into iced tea would become a worldwide sensation, but it did! These bubble teas (also called boba tea or pearl milk tea) started in Taiwan in the 1980s and began showing up in America in the 1990s. The basic drink is iced tea blended with milk and flavored syrups, and tapioca pearls at the bottom of the cup. Because bubble tea can be made with various teas, milks, and syrups, a well-stocked bubble tea shop could make as many as 250 different combinations.

Tea is the most consumed beverage in the world after water, and now with bubble teas, we have even more reason than ever to drink it.

In 1686, an English pamphlet listed twenty health benefits of tea, including "It Easeth the brain of heavy Damps" and "Strengthens Inward parts and Prevents Consumptions." Back then, tea was believed to be good for us, and modern medical studies agree.

The tea plant evolved chemical protections against insects, parasites, and bacteria, and those chemicals help us too. Some of those protective chemicals in tea are known as polyphenols. These strong antioxidants help prevent chronic illnesses including cancer. Tea, especially green tea, has been shown to be effective in supporting our immune systems. One type of polyphenols in tea, flavonoids, has been associated with the reduction of heart disease and may help lower the bad kind of cholesterol (low-density lipoprotein, or LDL).

All in all, tea is very good for us, except for the caffeine in it. The amount depends on the type of tea and the brewing method. In general, it has less than coffee, but may have more than soft drinks. While moderate amounts of caffeine are considered safe for adults, the American Association of Pediatrics does not recommend caffeine for children under the age of twelve.

TOP IT OFF

- Earl Grey tea is a black tea flavored with the oil of the bergamot orange. Legend has it that a Chinese tea master made it for the Earl of Grey, who was the prime minister of the United Kingdom from 1830 until 1834. His wife, Lady Grey, loved the tea so much, she had London tea merchants re-create it.
- China is the top producer of tea in the world, with India second and Kenya third.
- The top tea-drinking country is Turkey. They drink nearly seven pounds of tea per person a year. Ireland is second, and the United Kingdom is third. The United States is thirty-fifth in the rankings of tea-consuming countries.
- Herbal teas, such as chamomile, lavender, and ginger, are actually tisanes. Real tea only comes from the tea plant.

⁂ Concoction Corner ⁂

Tannins are just one of the many types of polyphenols found in tea, but the only ones that bind with iron in a chemical reaction known as chelation. Iron is important to our health because it helps our red blood cells carry oxygen. Because tannins bind with iron, it's recommended that people who are anemic shouldn't drink tea with their meals because the tea could affect iron absorption.

We can use the tannins in tea to see the iron that has been added to breakfast cereal.

TEA AS A MAGNET

YOU'LL NEED:

- 1 tea bag of a fairly strong black tea, such as English Breakfast
- 1 cup boiling water
- ½ cup iron-fortified breakfast cereal (read the label and find one with a lot of iron)
- ½ cup water
- Coffee filter
- Bowl
- White saucer

Place the tea bag in boiling water and let steep for five to ten minutes. The stronger, the better.

Blend the cereal and water in a blender until smooth. Pour the cereal mix into the coffee filter and let the water drain out into the bowl until there are a couple of tablespoons of strained liquid. This might take several minutes. Take the filter filled with cereal mush out of the bowl. Slowly pour about ¼ cup of tea into the strained liquid while stirring. Let it settle for a minute or two. Then spoon out some of the tea, getting as much as you can from the bottom of the bowl, and pour into a shallow saucer. When the tannins and iron bind together, it will appear as dark specks in the liquid.

Chapter Four

WAKE UP!

WHEN THEODORE ROOSEVELT WAS ONLY FIVE YEARS OLD, his parents made him drink coffee. In 1863, coffee was the most prescribed treatment for asthma and little Teddy had it bad. As he grew up, his coffee habit grew with him. By the time he became the twenty-sixth president of the United States, he drank a gallon a day.

Roosevelt wasn't the only legendary java lover. The composer Ludwig van Beethoven had one cup every day made with exactly sixty beans. He counted them to be sure. The author of *The Wonderful Wizard of Oz,* L. Frank Baum, had at least five cups with cream and sugar every morning before starting to work on his book.

Coffee has been captivating people for more than a thousand years. According to legend, the first coffee craver was Kaldi, a young Ethiopian goat herder.

Every day, Kaldi led his goats into the hills so they could graze. One afternoon, he whistled for them. Normally they came trotting out of the forest, but not this time. He looked all over and found them prancing and bleating like they were at a party.

He noticed they were also eating little red berries from a tree. Since the

goats didn't seem to be sick, Kaldi thought it would be safe for him to try one. A few minutes after chewing the berry, energy surged through his body. He felt amazing! He ran back to his village to spread the word about the fantastic tree.

Eventually people learned that the beans inside the cherry-looking berry were the important part. They also began trading them with the Arabs across the Red Sea. Sometime in the fifteenth century, instead of grinding the beans and eating them, holy men in Yemen began steeping them in water. They drank the beverage to help them stay awake during late-night prayers. News about their brew got out and coffee spread through the Arab world.

Europeans traveling to the Middle East in the early 1600s noticed the Arab obsession with coffee. It didn't take long for Europeans to figure out why the Arabs liked it so much. By the mid-1600s, coffeehouses began to open in London, Paris, and Rome.

CRADLE OF COFFEE AND HUMANS

Ethiopia is not only the birthplace of coffee, but it's also believed to be the birthplace of the human species. In 1974, one of the oldest fossils of an early hominid species (*Australopithecus afarensis*) was found in the Danakil Depression in Ethiopia. The skeleton, named Lucy, is estimated to be 3.2 million years old.

Coffee Hero

The first coffeehouse in Vienna opened in 1683 by Georg Franz Kolschitzky, a war hero with a sensitive nose.

Vienna was in trouble. The Turkish army had surrounded the city and was preparing to attack. The Viennese needed help from the Polish army but had no way to get word to them. Kolschitzky had spent time in Turkey and could speak the language, so he volunteered for a dangerous mission. Disguised as a Turkish soldier, he sneaked through enemy lines and delivered the message. The Polish army ambushed the Turks from behind. Shocked and scared, they jumped on their camels and ran away, leaving their stuff behind.

The Viennese built a huge fire and dumped the Turks' trash on it, including sacks of brown pellets that they thought might be camel kibble. Kolschitzky

smelled a familiar aroma. He rushed to the bonfire and pulled the sacks to safety. Since the Viennese didn't know what to do with the stuff, they gave all five hundred bags of coffee to Kolschitzky as a reward for saving the city. He couldn't drink all that by himself, so he opened a café.

Europe Wakes Up

Before coffee and tea came to Europe, people drank beer, wine, and cider all day long because they didn't trust the water. The alcohol made them feel dull and drowsy. When they finally tried caffeine, it blew their minds. They felt alert and invigorated, and ideas bounced around their brains like Kaldi's goats.

They wanted to share their brilliant thoughts with others, so they met in coffeehouses to get caffeinated and discuss the important topics of the times. In London, these coffeehouses were nicknamed "Penny Universities" because for a penny cup, you could hear lectures from some of the brightest minds in town, including Benjamin Franklin. When he lived in London, he hung out at his favorite coffeehouse so much, his mail was delivered there.

Benjamin Franklin was in England trying to help with the tense situation between the British Parliament and the American colonies over the tea tax. (Learn more about the Boston Tea Party in chapter two.) Because of the tax, Americans boycotted tea and drank coffee instead. After the Revolutionary War, tea became acceptable again, but it never regained its former status. The new United States of America was a coffee country. By the late 1800s, Americans consumed nearly half of all the coffee produced in the world.

HOW CAFFEINE KEEPS US AWAKE

As we go about our day, the neurotransmitter adenosine starts building up in our brain and locking into its specific receptor sites. When enough adenosine locks in, the brain knows it's time to go to sleep. Caffeine sneaks into adenosine's receptor sites and blocks them. Our brain thinks everything is great and keeps on working at full speed.

Westward Ho!

Caffeine doesn't just stimulate the brain, it also fights fatigue, which is exactly what cowboys needed in the Wild West. Herding cattle meant hours in the saddle, and they needed all the energy they could get. No wimpy sugar or cream for these tough hombres. They liked it painfully hot and strong enough to "float a horseshoe." If the cook gave them a weak brew, they chewed them out for serving "belly wash" or "brown gargle."

Gold miners needed stamina too. When they came to town for supplies, coffee was on their shopping list. Most people who got rich during the gold rush were the shopkeepers, not the miners. So, it was very wise of young fourteen-year-old James Folger to get a job in a coffee company instead of prospecting like his two older brothers. The three of them had come to San Francisco from Massachusetts in 1849, hoping to strike it rich.

His brothers gave up after a while and went back East, but James stayed in the store. He eventually bought the company and renamed it J. A. Folger & Co. Although it's not owned by the Folger family anymore, the brand is still popular today.

GOLD FEVER

On January 24, 1848, James Wilson Marshall found gold nuggets in the river by Sutter's Mill near San Francisco, California. News spread quickly, and over one hundred thousand hopeful prospectors swarmed into the area. But they didn't get there quickly. Going across the country by land could take six months. Traveling by ship wasn't much faster. Sailing from the East Coast to the West Coast took about four months because the ship had to go around the tip of South America. Even though the rush started in 1848, most prospectors didn't arrive in California until 1849, hence the nickname "the 49ers."

✳✳ Like a Fine Wine ✳✳

Folgers, and other brands, such as Chase & Sanborn and Hills Bros., liked to brag about the quality of their coffee beans in advertisements. But they really had no clue if their beans were good or not. They bought them from wholesalers who priced them on size alone. This bothered Clarence Bickford, a coffee bean wholesaler in San Francisco, because he believed that flavor could be affected by many things and bigger was not always better. He developed a method of testing the quality of coffee similar to how wine was judged. The Hills brothers were one of the first to adopt Bickford's "cup-tasting" method in the 1880s.

FROM *COFFEA* TO CUP

The two main kinds of coffee trees, *Coffea arabica* and *Coffea robusta*, are grown in a zone around the equator called the Coffee Belt. Weather and soil conditions affect the quality of the coffee. It takes a young tree four years to produce its first crop of cherries, and it can take those cherries several months to ripen from green to bright red. Each cherry contains two seeds (beans) encased in a sticky pulp. After the beans are separated from the cherry, they're dried and hulled. At this point, the beans are called "green coffee" and are ready to be roasted.

Now known simply as cupping—the tasters are called cuppers—the process starts with several deep sniffs to capture the aroma of the coffee.

Then, the cupper sucks the liquid into their mouth with loud, slow slurps. After several swishes around the mouth, they spit it out into their handy-dandy spittoon. If there were table manner police, cuppers would get a ticket every time. Today, almost all coffee companies employ a professional cupper for quality control.

✳✳ Quantity over Quality ✳✳

For a while coffee quality improved, but World War I changed that. Soldiers didn't care what their coffee tasted like. They just wanted it hot, strong, and often.

Thankfully for them, instant coffee had been invented in 1910 by George Washington (not related to our first president). With these dried coffee crystals, soldiers could easily stir up a cup, no grinders or pots needed. The army bought all of Washington's inventory when the United States entered World War I in 1918. The Nestlé company, of chocolate fame, improved the process of drying coffee to crystals and came out with Nescafé in 1938 in time for World War II.

After these wars, soldiers came home with their taste buds tuned to instant. Even if they wanted better flavor, they were unlikely to get it because the most common way to make coffee at the time was with a percolator.

Invented by Hanson Goodrich in 1889, this stove-top coffee pot had a tube in the middle with a filter basket for the coffee grounds in the upper part. As the water in the bottom got hot, it rose through the tube, sprayed over the grounds, and dripped through, over and over again. To say that it was overcooked would be an understatement.

Percolated or instant coffee tasted okay to older Americans. After two world wars and the Great Depression, they weren't picky. But their java didn't jibe with the next generation. The baby boomers (people born between 1946 and 1964) were choosing ice-cold colas over a cup of bitter brew. In the 1960s, the consumption of coffee per person went down for the first time since the Revolutionary War, while consumption of soft drinks went up.

Americans Like Coffee a Latte Again

When Alfred Peet, the son of a Dutch coffee roaster, came to the United States in 1955, he understood why baby boomers were reaching for colas. Between the under-roasted, poor-quality beans used in most grocery store brands and the percolators boiling the flavor out, coffee tasted terrible!

Peet set out to educate Americans on what a good cup of coffee should taste like. In 1966, he opened a shop in Berkeley, California, selling high-quality, finely roasted beans for home brewing. He served free samples and soon had a line of customers out the door waiting to buy a bag of his perfectly roasted beans.

Three of Peet's fans, Gordon Bowker, Zev Siegl, and Jerry Baldwin, opened their own specialty coffee roasting shop in Seattle, Washington, in 1971.

They named their new business after a character in *Moby Dick*. Can you guess the name? That's right! Starbucks!

PERCOLATORS PUSHED OUT

In October 1972, the simply named Mr. Coffee hit the market. This automatic drip machine made coffee by dripping boiling water directly onto the coffee grounds, which then seeped through to the carafe. Not only did it produce a pot quicker than a percolator, but the coffee also tasted better. Within a couple of years, over five million automatic drip makers had been sold and percolators were a thing of the past. Although Mr. Coffee was a huge improvement, John Sylvan thought it would be great if people could make a fresh cup of coffee whenever they wanted it, one cup at a time. It took years of tinkering with prototypes, but finally Sylvan and his partner, Peter Dragone, came up with a working model of the Keurig for offices in 1998. Home versions came out in 2004 and are now in more than thirty-three million homes. *Keurig* is a Dutch word meaning "excellence."

The first location did so well, they opened six more. In 1982, they hired New Yorker Howard Schultz to be their marketing manager. Schultz had big ideas for growing the company. He had been inspired after a trip to Milan, Italy, where he saw how successful espresso cafés were there. In Italy, espresso cafés were the center of social life for everyone from teenagers on their first date to businesspeople making deals. Schultz believed that Americans would welcome a casual meeting place too. Unfortunately, the owners of Starbucks didn't share Schultz's vision and wouldn't change from selling coffee beans by the pound to selling coffee by the cup.

ITALIAN–THE COFFEE DRINK LANGUAGE

- **ESPRESSO** is produced by forcing highly pressurized hot water through very finely ground beans to produce a cup of concentrated coffee in a few seconds. *Espresso* means "fast" or "express." Coffee drinks with Italian names use espresso as the base.

- **CAPPUCCINO** has one or two shots of espresso with an equal layer of steamed milk and topped with frothed milk. The ratio of espresso to milk is one to one. The drink gets its name because the color matches the robes worn by Capuchin monks and literally means "little Capuchin."

- **CAFFE LATTE** has a ratio of two milks to one espresso and the steamed milk is mixed in with a thin layer of frothed milk on top. *Caffe latte* literally means "coffee milk."

- **MACCHIATO** means "spotted" or "stained," so there is just a spot of steamed milk added to a shot of espresso.

- **AMERICANO** is espresso with added water so that it tastes more like a regularly brewed cup of coffee that Americans prefer.

- **BARISTA** means "bartender" because an Italian coffee shop is called a *bar*.

In 1987, Schultz finally got his chance to buy Starbucks. He immediately transformed the stores into cafés modeled after the ones he'd seen in Milan, which included calling the servers *baristas* and using Italian words such as *venti, grande,* and *macchiato.* Schultz was right. Americans did love the café scene.

Schultz didn't even need to advertise very much. Just the sight of other people carrying a cup with the iconic mermaid logo was enough to draw new customers. Some Starbucks investors thought Schultz was foolish to open a location in Los Angeles in 1990. Who wanted hot coffee in hot weather? But as soon as a few movie stars were seen carrying a Starbucks cup, everyone wanted to be seen with one.

Americans have totally embraced the coffee shop culture and not just at Starbucks. In 1990, there were approximately six hundred coffee shops in the United States. Thirty years later, there are over thirty-five thousand. Coffee shops prove that it's not just the caffeine that people were craving, but the social connections too.

However, people were also craving variety. Back in the days of a ten-cent cup of coffee at the diner, you could get your coffee with sugar or cream or black. Now, you can choose hot, iced, lattes, cappuccinos, flavorings, toppings, syrups, milks, and more. There are over fifty-five thousand ways to order a beverage at Starbucks.

Coffee sure has come a long way from Kaldi's little red berries.

Even though there's no way coffee could be a substitute for an asthma inhaler, caffeine does help open airways. It's also helpful for migraines and constipation. Coffee is a good source of antioxidants and has been shown to reduce the risk of heart disease, stroke, Alzheimer's, and type 2 diabetes. But it can also cause insomnia, anxiety, and jitters and raise blood pressure. Before you pour another cup, keep in mind the recommended maximum amounts of caffeine for adults is a maximum of 300 to 400 milligrams per day and for young people (ages thirteen to eighteen) only 100 milligrams per day. On average, a cup of coffee has 90 to 110 milligrams of caffeine. The American Academy of Pediatrics (AAP) recommends that children under twelve avoid caffeine completely because it is addictive and children are more likely to suffer from withdrawal symptoms including headaches, fatigue, and irritability.

TOP IT OFF

- In 1732, Johann Sebastian Bach wrote *Coffee Cantata,* a humorous piece in which a daughter begs her father not to take her coffee away.
- Caffeine is one of a group of natural chemicals called alkaloids. Scientists believe caffeine evolved in plants as insecticides. A few chomps on a coffee bean and it's bye-bye beetle.
- Kopi luwak, the most expensive coffee in the world, sells for $35 to $100 a cup. It's made from beans that have been partially digested by the Asian palm civet, a small catlike animal in Indonesia. It's also called "cat poop coffee."
- It might seem like Americans drink a lot of coffee, but not compared to the Dutch. They drink an average of 18 pounds of coffee per person a year, putting them at number one in consumption. Americans rank fourteenth with an average of 7.7 pounds a year.

☀☀ Concoction Corner ☀☀

After discovering coffee, the ancient Ethiopians used it in many ways, including mixing it with animal fat for a high-energy snack. This super simple recipe uses that concept of infusing coffee into food for extra flavor. Want to avoid caffeine? No worries. It tastes just as good with decaf.

CHILI CON COFFEE

YOU'LL NEED:

- 1 pound lean ground beef
- 1 cup chopped onion
- 2 cloves garlic, minced
- 1 cup brewed coffee (decaf or regular)
- 1 (14.5-ounce) can diced tomatoes with green chiles
- 1 (14.5-ounce) can diced tomatoes
- 1½ teaspoons chili powder
- ½ teaspoon pepper
- 1 teaspoon salt
- 1 (15-ounce) can each of pinto beans, kidney beans, great northern beans

In a large pot, cook the ground beef, onion, and garlic until browned. Drain the grease. Stir in the rest of the ingredients. Bring to a boil. Cover and reduce heat to low and simmer for 25 to 30 minutes. Serve with sour cream and grated cheddar cheese.

Chapter Five

THERE'S NO CREAM IN CREAM SODA

IN ALMOST EVERY CULTURE, ANCIENT PEOPLE BELIEVED THAT the mysterious bubbles popping out of mineral springs had magical healing powers. They didn't know that those bubbles were just gases because they didn't know what gases were.

Over two thousand years ago, the Greeks theorized that everything in the world was made from four basic elements—water, earth, fire, and air. That concept didn't get challenged until the 1500s, when scientists began to question if there might be more to air than previously thought.

The list of gas-obsessed scientists is a long one and includes Jan Baptista van Helmont from Belgium, who coined the word "gas" in the early 1600s. The English team fielded such legendary greats as Joseph Black, Henry Cavendish, and Robert Boyle. We certainly can't forget the French chemist Antoine Lavoisier, whose valuable work in chemistry was ended by a guillotine in 1794 during the French Revolution. But that's a story for another book.

Another brilliant Brit, Joseph Priestley, conducted a series of experiments in the 1770s proving that air consisted of different gases, and it wasn't one pure substance as the Greeks believed. He isolated one gas, which he called "dephlogisticated air." Thankfully for poor spellers everywhere, Lavoisier renamed it "oxygen" in 1778.

Although discovering oxygen is pretty cool, it was Priestley's experiments with carbon dioxide that earned him the title of Father of Carbonated Drinks. He lived next door to a brewery in Leeds, England, in the early 1770s. The bubbles erupting from the fermenting vats of beer fascinated him.

He tried to capture those bubbles. While standing over the simmering vats, he poured water between two glasses over and over again as fast as he could. It worked! The gas dissolved in the liquid. Priestley had made the first artificial carbonated water.

Later, he devised an easier method of producing carbon dioxide using chalk and oil of vitriol, which he captured with a system of glass jars and tubes. In 1772, he published *Directions for Impregnating Water with Fixed Air, in Order to Communicate to It the Peculiar Spirit and Virtues of Pyrmont Water, and Other Mineral Waters of a Similar Nature.*

JOSEPH PRIESTLEY (1733-1804)

Born in Birstall, England, Joseph Priestley studied to be a minister. Besides religion, his other interests included chemistry, electricity, botany, and politics. He published over 150 works in these subjects. His first scientific paper, "The History of Electricity," was published in 1767 with encouragement from his friend Benjamin Franklin. Priestley immigrated to the United States in 1794 and settled in Pennsylvania.

At the time, Pyrmont Water, which came from a naturally effervescent spring in Germany, was imported into England for use as a medicine. That Priestley could make it in a laboratory was huge! In spite of having the longest title of the year, his paper won the prestigious Copley Medal from the Royal Society.

The medical community truly believed carbonation cured diseases. Priestley thought so too. He specifically hoped that his fizzy water would prevent scurvy in sailors. It didn't of course. Only vitamin C could do that.

Because carbonated water was supposed to be a medicine, drugstore owners began to sell it. One of the first was an English apothecary, Thomas Henry, who sold it in his shop in 1781. As more pharmacists began making carbonated water, or soda water, the methods and equipment improved. In 1809, Joseph Hawkins in Philadelphia made the first soda fountain when he attached a faucet to his soda-making machine. By the 1820s, drugstores all over the country had a version of Hawkins's soda-dispensing fountain.

Making bubbles proved to be easy. All the pharmacists needed was an acid and a carbonate. The name "soda water" came from the early use of bicarbonate of soda, but other materials worked too. John Matthews developed a machine that used sulfuric acid and marble chips. When construction began in St. Patrick's Cathedral in New York City in 1858, Matthews bought the leftover marble for his soda machine. It's estimated that twenty-five million gallons of soda water came from St. Patrick's scraps during its twenty-year construction period.

MARBLE'S CALCIUM CARBONATE

Calcium carbonate ($CaCO_3$) reacts with acids to produce carbon dioxide. Commonly found in chalk, limestone, and marble, it makes up 4 percent of Earth's crust. This versatile substance is used as a binder in medical pills and tablets. Because it's white, it's also used as a filler in concrete, paints, and paper.

✳✳ Sodalicious ✳✳

After a while, people got bored with plain old soda water, so drugstore clerks started adding flavors. Some of the additives were intended as medicines, too, such as ginger, but some were just for the taste, like chocolate. The flavors were made into syrups so they would mix into the water easier. Drugstores offered hundreds of flavored syrups from the basics like strawberry, lemon, and vanilla to weirder ones like coriander, quince, and crushed violets.

Going to the drugstore for a soda became a social event, especially in the summer when customers craved a refreshing, icy, fizzy drink. As competition for customers got tighter, the soda fountains got more elegant and more elaborate. The frenzy for the fanciest fountain inspired James W. Tufts's thirty-foot-tall Arctic Soda Fountain, which was displayed at the 1876 Philadelphia World's Fair. By 1895, fifty thousand soda fountains flowed in America.

The soda jerks (the nickname of the servers because of the way they jerked the syrup dispensers) constantly created new flavor combinations to keep the customers coming back. One week, customers could choose drinks with names like Foam Fun, Silver Float, and Ginger Ciz, and the next week, Poet's Dream, Pineapple Smash, or Gardner's Nightcap would be on the menu.

With so many to choose from, it was rare when one bubbled up above the rest and lasted long enough to make a name for itself, but that's exactly what happened with Dr Pepper.

The oldest major American soft drink brand got its humble start in Waco, Texas, at the Old Corner Drug Store in 1885. It was concocted by Charles Alderton, a young pharmacist who enjoyed fiddling with flavors at the soda fountain in his free time. Owner Wade Morrison liked Alderton's blend and put it on the menu. Customers ordered it by saying, "Shoot me a Waco."

HOT SUMMER, COLD DRINKS

Americans had a hankering for cold drinks long before they had refrigerators or ice makers. In the 1800s, ice companies devised a way to supply the chill. During the winter months, they cut blocks of ice out of frozen lakes and stored them in special double-walled warehouses. Sawdust acted as insulation by filling the spaces between the walls. Companies painted the outside of the buildings white to reflect the sunlight, and they insulated their delivery wagons. While these things helped, they couldn't completely stop the ice from melting. By the time summer deliveries began, half of the ice would be gone.

Morrison realized that they were on to something when other drugstores wanted to buy their syrup. Alderton got tired of making sodas and went back to being a pharmacist, so in 1891, Morrison partnered with R. S. Lazenby to start bottling their booming beverage. But it needed a name.

There are almost as many stories about how Dr Pepper got its name as there are fruit flavors in the formula. One story suggests Morrison named it after Dr. Charles T. Pepper because he had a crush on the doctor's daughter and wanted to impress her. Another story features a freckle-faced employee nicknamed "Pepper." The addition of "Dr" helped the drink sound healthy. A really wacky theory claims it was named after Queen Elizabeth's personal physician. Morrison never revealed the secret of the name.

After taking Texas by storm, Dr Pepper debuted to the world at the St. Louis World's Fair in 1904, and it's been our "friendly Pepper-upper" ever since.

Where's the Cream?

Another flavor that stood the test of time was cream soda. But unlike Dr Pepper's distinctive flavor, cream sodas varied from one recipe to another and from one soda fountain to another. One of the earliest mentions of "cream soda" was in 1852. E. M. Sheldon printed a recipe in the *Michigan Farmer* that included cream of tartar, salt, sugar, milk, and an egg. Some recipes didn't include milk at all, leading to the theory that the term "cream" might have been referring to the cream of tartar.

Other food historians believe the "cream" in cream sodas was ice cream. Robert Green of Philadelphia claimed to be the first to add ice cream to a soda water in 1872. Whether he was the first or not, ice cream sodas did become one of the top-selling treats at drugstore soda fountains.

The customer would choose which syrup flavor they wanted. Then the soda jerk would mix up the soda in a glass and plop in a dollop of vanilla ice cream.

When soft drink manufacturers wanted to bottle cream sodas, the ice cream melted out of the recipe and was replaced with vanilla. Studies have shown that vanilla triggers our taste buds to perceive a creamy sensation even when there is no milk.

While cream sodas might not rank as high as colas in the beverage popularity charts, there are still hundreds of brands available in the market today, which is a tribute to the longevity of this classic. Cream sodas come in different colors and flavors. The Big Red brand is red with hints of lemon and orange, while the Frostie brand is blue. Sprecher Cream Soda from Milwaukee, Wisconsin, is sweetened with caramelized honey. But what they all share is vanilla.

One of the earliest brands is Dr. Brown's, which has been around since 1869. According to legend, Dr. Brown made health tonics and sold them door to door in New York City. His first was a celery tonic that he created to treat malnourished children. Then he added ginger ale, root beer, and cream soda, and they all supposedly cured various ailments. In 1886, Dr. Brown asked the Schoneberger & Noble company to help him bottle and sell his beverages. Then, the mysterious Dr. Brown faded away like Bigfoot into the forest. We don't even know his first name.

Bottling Bubbles

We can't talk about sodas without mentioning the Father of the Soft Drink Industry, Jacob Schweppe. He was the first to manufacture and bottle a carbonated beverage on a large scale in 1783.

Although he trained to be a silversmith and jewelry maker, Schweppe was obsessed with gas. He studied the work of Joseph Priestley and Antoine Lavoisier and devoted himself to devising a way to mass produce carbonated water. After lots of tinkering, he finally created a system that worked.

WHY DO SODAS MAKE US BURP?

Soda manufacturers use high pressure to dissolve carbon dioxide into the liquid. Then it's immediately sealed in a can or bottle. When we pop the top, the pressure releases suddenly and the carbon dioxide escapes with a *whoosh*. The rest of the gas goes into our stomach when we drink it. The gas wants to escape from there too! It forces its way up our esophagus and out of our mouths as a burp.

He began selling bottled soda water in Geneva, Switzerland, in 1783. Sales were so good he opened a second factory in London in 1792. In the beginning, his company sold only carbonated water. The famous Schweppes ginger ale was introduced in 1870.

Schweppe designed a special oval-shaped bottle with flat sides for his fizzy water. He intended for the bottles to be stored on their sides so the liquid would keep the corks moist and the seal intact. Because they looked like squished eggs, some people called his waters "egg sodas."

This special design was handmade by a glassblower, but so were all the other bottles. There wasn't an automated way to manufacture glass yet.

An experienced glassblower could make about 200 bottles a day, which wasn't nearly enough for all the beverage companies that needed them.

Finally in 1904, Michael Owens unstopped the glass supply chain by inventing the automated bottle making machine. Instead of 200 bottles a day, Owens's machine could produce 240 bottles a minute! In less than fifteen years, more than two hundred Owens machines operated around the country.

The bottle was only half the challenge. The other half was sealing it so the bubbles didn't escape. For more than four hundred years, the most common method of sealing a bottle used a cork plug. Unfortunately, the cork sometimes dried out and shrunk, then the liquid leaked. Inventors raced to create a better bottle stopper. There were over 1,500 patents for bottle tops before 1900.

In 1879, Charles G. Hutchinson created a stopper that used a gasket hanging inside the bottle and attached to a wire. To seal the bottle, a person pulled the gasket up by the wire. To unseal the stopper, a person smacked the top, which released the pressure and made a loud *pop*. If you ever wondered why we call them "soda pops," that's why.

Although Hutchinson's cap was the industry favorite for years, it was difficult to install and clumsy to use. In 1892, William Painter invented a simple metal cap lined with cork. Using a special crimping machine, the cap would be squeezed tight around the mouth of the bottle.

His "crown cap" was so simple that no one believed it would work. To prove it, Painter capped cases of bottles and shipped them to South America and back. After months at sea, not one of them had leaked, exploded, or broken! Bottling companies crowned the new cap the new champ!

As bottling and capping methods improved, more people began buying their favorite soft drinks at grocery stores. Because of that and the growing suburban communities with indoor shopping malls and food courts, the allure of the downtown soda fountain faded away. But Americans' love of sodas didn't fade away. Except for bottled water, Americans buy more soft drinks than any other beverage, even more than coffee.

QUIRKY CORK

Because it's lightweight, resistant to fire and insects, and impermeable to gas and liquid, cork is used in many products, including bottle stoppers, flooring materials, wall tiles, and badminton shuttlecocks. It's harvested by stripping the outer layer of bark from the cork tree *(Quercus suber)*. The tree must be at least twenty-five years old before its first stripping and it takes about nine years for it to grow back. The top cork producing countries are Portugal, Algeria, Spain, and Morocco.

OH NO! NUTRITION

It's ironic that sodas were originally sold in drugstores as a medicine, because now they have been associated with the increase of obesity and its related diseases. Consumption of soft drinks went up from 90 (eight-ounce) servings per American in 1942 to 618 (eight-ounce) servings in 2019.

The *Dietary Guidelines for Americans 2020–2025* recommends that added sugars be no more than 10 percent of a person's daily calories. It's estimated that the average American gets 16 percent of their calories from sugar, with nearly half that those coming from soft drinks.

Back in the day of the drugstore soda fountains, soft drinks were a special treat. It would be healthier if we thought of them that way again.

TOP IT OFF

- Most American cream soda brands are caramel colored, but Australians expect theirs to be bright yellow and Canadians prefer pink.
- In the 1994 movie *Forrest Gump,* Forrest drinks fifteen Dr Peppers while waiting to meet President John F. Kennedy.
- According to Guinness World Records, Italian Michele Forgione (who competes under the name Rutt Mysterio) set the record for the longest burp on June 16, 2009, with a time of 1 minute 13 seconds.
- Charles Leiper Grigg introduced "Bib-Label Lithiated Lemon-Lime Soda" in October 1929. That shortened to "7Up" in 1936. The drink contained lithium (a mood-stabilizing drug) until 1948.

⁎⁎ Concoction Corner ⁎⁎

Make your own carbonated water with this fun experiment.

BALLOON BUBBLE-UP

. . . .

YOU'LL NEED:

- Funnel
- Balloon
- ⅓ cup baking soda
- 1 cup vinegar
- 16 to 20-ounce empty plastic bottle
- Bowl of water

Use the funnel to fill the balloon with the baking soda.

Pour the vinegar into the plastic bottle.

While pinching the neck of the balloon shut so the baking soda doesn't come out, stretch the balloon over the mouth of the bottle.

Once it is attached, allow the baking soda to fall into the bottle and vinegar.

When the balloon is inflated, slip it off the bottle and pinch it shut quickly with your fingers. Hold the balloon under the water in the bowl. With one hand holding the inflated part of the balloon, let go of the other end, and watch as the gas permeates the water and bubbles to the top.

WHY THIS HAPPENS

. . . .

Baking soda is a base, and the vinegar contains acetic acid. When mixed, the hydrogen ions in the vinegar react with the sodium and bicarbonate ions in the baking soda, making carbonic acid and sodium acetate. Then the carbonic acid breaks down into water and carbon dioxide.

Chapter Six

AT THE ROOT OF IT

THERE'S NO BEER IN ROOT BEER AND THERE'S NO ALE IN ginger ale . . . anymore. But there used to be. Originally, ginger ale and root beer contained alcohol because they were fermented. However, they didn't have a lot of alcohol, so the whole family drank them, even the kids! They were considered to be not only safe, but downright healthy. Doctors prescribed ginger ale for upset stomachs and root beer for almost everything else.

When the temperance movement heated up in America in the late 1800s, beverage companies rushed to put nonalcoholic products on the market. Because root beer and ginger ale could be made without fermentation, they became alcohol-free, but no one bothered to change their names. These supposedly healthy and certainly tasty tonics were soft drinks stars in the early 1900s.

SASSY SASSAFRAS

The *Sassafras albidum* tree is indigenous to North America and averages thirty to fifty feet tall. Native Americans had a vast knowledge of herbal medicines, and one of the most versatile plants in their medicine chest was sassafras. The leaves, roots, and bark are all fragrant and were used for cooking and medicines. The Cherokee used sassafras to treat fever, diarrhea, and rheumatism. The Iroquois also used it for tapeworms, sore eyes, and nosebleeds. The Rappahannock crushed the leaves into a paste to cover burn wounds.

 Which Root?

It's easy to guess what ginger ale is made of, but what is root beer made of? That depends on who's making it. The term "root beer" began showing up in the mid-1800s, but that type of brewed beverage had been around for a couple of hundred years before that. Every household had their own recipe, and they used whatever spices, herbs, berries, barks, and roots they could find.

The English made their "small beers" with a variety of plants including ginger, lemon, and the barks of birch and spruce trees. When they settled in America, they learned from the Native Americans that the aromatic roots of the sassafras tree made delicious beverages and useful medicines.

Sir Francis Drake took sassafras back to England from the Virginia colonies in 1586. When the English learned about sassafras's medicinal reputation, they went gaga over it. They tried it for every ailment from toothaches to tuberculosis. Some people even claimed it cured old age! By the mid-1600s, sassafras was second only to tobacco as the top export from the Americas to England.

While the English settled the northeastern part of America, the Spanish called dibs on the southern part. They found the Seminoles using sarsaparilla as a medicine and spice. The wonderfully smelling sarsaparilla vine (*Smilax pumila*) thrives in the sandy soils of southern coastal states such as Louisiana, Texas, and Florida. The Spanish explorers thought they had hit the gold mine of medicines and took it back to Spain. They liked how it tasted in their teas too.

Cure-Alls

With the public already believing sassafras and sarsaparilla were wonder cures, it was inevitable they would become ingredients in patent medicines. In 1858, James C. Ayer introduced his Ayer's Sarsaparilla and advertised it as a tonic to cure ulcers, pimples, tumors, dropsy, dyspepsia, and all diseases caused by "impure blood," which back then meant almost everything. This miraculous medicine sold for one dollar a bottle ($31 in today's money). Ayer's sarsaparilla tonic, his cough medicine, and his hair tonic earned $20 million (over $400 million in today's money), making Ayer one of the most successful patent-medicine makers ever.

For those who couldn't afford to buy expensive patent medicines, Dr. A. W. Chase published his book of recipes in 1870 so people could make tonics at home. His recipe for root beer included both sassafras and sarsaparilla, plus a few other plants. He recommended that families make it every spring and "drink freely of it for several weeks and thereby save, perhaps several dollars in doctors' bills." According to him, this root beer was much better than an apple a day to keep the doctor away.

Making root beer at home was easier said than done. First, all the ingredients had to be gathered. Then they had to be cleaned, chopped, boiled, strained, and, finally, bottled. When Charles E. Hires developed instant root beer in 1876, he made a lot of people happy. He blended sixteen roots and berries and then concentrated it into a dry powder. A twenty-five-cent packet made five gallons of root beer, which was cheaper than buying all the individual ingredients and half the work.

A savvy marketer, he advertised in newspapers and magazines with bold claims such as "the greatest health-giving beverage in the whole world." He got national exposure by handing out free samples at the Philadelphia World's Fair in 1876, and soon Hires Root Beer was a household name. In 1893, he began selling his ready-to-drink root beer in bottles.

✳✳ Better than Booze ✳✳

A deeply religious man, Hires totally supported the temperance movement. He advertised his root beer as "a temperance drink of the highest medicinal value." He wanted to call it Hires' Root Tea, but a friend convinced him that manly men wouldn't drink anything with "tea" in the name. It came as a total shock to Hires when in 1895, a chemical analysis of his root beer determined it contained alcohol. The Women's Christian Temperance Union (WCTU) were surprised and angry because they had promoted root beer as a family-friendly beverage. They called for a total boycott.

Hires fought back. He got a second analysis done by a different chemist, and it proved that his root beer didn't have any more alcohol than a loaf of bread. He blasted ads in all the newspapers with the new test results. The WCTU backed down and canceled the boycott.

With Hires Root Beer selling so well, others wanted to cash in on the craze. Barq's entered the market in 1898, A&W in 1919, and Dad's in 1937. That's just to name a few. There have been more than eight hundred brands of root beer since Hires began in 1876.

Over time, people realized that root beer wasn't a magical cure-all, but they kept drinking it anyway because they liked it. Then a terrible discovery almost shut down the root beer industry forever. In 1960, research revealed that safrole (the main chemical compound in sassafras) caused liver cancer in laboratory rats. The Food and Drug Administration (FDA) banned it. The root beer companies had to scramble and come up with new recipes without sassafras, relying on sarsaparilla, wintergreen, cloves, and anise instead.

After that scare, Americans didn't favor root beer as much. At one time, root beer was one of the top-selling soda flavors in the country. Now it makes up only about 5 percent of soft drink sales. While that may not seem very high, it's higher than anywhere else. Except for a couple of brands in Canada and Australia, root beer is found only in America. Apparently, people from other countries think root beer tastes worse than cough syrup.

THE TEMPERANCE MOVEMENT AND PROHIBITION

In the 1800s, America was a boozy place. Almost everyone drank alcohol in some form, even children. A movement grew, mainly among religious groups, to encourage people to stop drinking alcohol (temperance). One of the largest, the Women's Christian Temperance Union, formed in 1874. They, and the other organizations, pushed for making the manufacture, sale, and import of alcohol illegal. After many attempts, they finally succeeded when Congress passed the National Prohibition Act (also known as the Volstead Act), which went into effect on January 17, 1920. Although it did help reduce the consumption of alcohol, it also inspired "bootlegging," a nickname for illegally making and selling whiskey. When the crime wave got to be too much, Congress repealed the Prohibition Act in February 1933. States could continue to ban alcohol if they wanted, but it was no longer a national law.

Spiced Right

For over five thousand years, ginger has graced kitchens and medicine cabinets throughout Asia and India. When other cultures discovered its unique flavor and healing properties, ginger spread across the globe. It was so valuable in the 1300s, Europeans would trade a whole sheep for one pound of ginger.

Long hailed as a miracle drug, ginger was a natural addition to American soda fountain menus in the early days when fizzy soda waters doubled as health tonics. Even though ginger was a popular drink flavor in the states, it was an Irishman that bottled it first.

ZINGIBER OFFICINALE–ALSO KNOWN AS GINGER

Ginger is in the Zingiberaceae family of plants, which includes turmeric and cardamom. It's not a root, but an underground stem called a rhizome. The green leafy part grows aboveground to a height of three or four feet. Ginger thrives in subtropical areas with temperatures above fifty degrees. India is the top producer of ginger, with China being second.

Dr. Thomas Cantrell began his career in a chemist shop in Belfast, Ireland, in 1849. He must have liked soft drinks more than medicines because he fiddled around with flavors until he got his ginger ale recipe right. He opened his own shop in 1852 and started selling bottled ginger ale, lemonade, and soda water. In 1866, his firm started exporting to America, where it quickly became a favorite for those who could get it. He later merged his company with Henry Cochrane to become Cantrell and Cochrane.

Meanwhile in Detroit, Michigan, the young James Vernor started his career in a pharmacy in 1858. He had been experimenting with ginger syrups when the Civil War broke out. Before he left to fight, he stored his latest syrup in a wooden cask. When he returned four years later, it had aged to perfection.

It took him a year to get production up and running and, in 1866, he started selling it. When hospitals figured out that Vernor's Ginger Ale soothed their patients' upset stomachs, they became some of his best customers.

Canadian John James McLaughlin believed ginger ale would be his path to fame and fortune. In an obvious attempt at capturing some of the Cantrell's customers, he started selling McLaughlin's Belfast Style Ginger Ale in 1894. Not completely satisfied with his product, he kept tinkering with the recipe to make it lighter and less sweet. Finally, in 1905, he filed a patent for his new formula and trademarked it Canada Dry Pale Ginger Ale. By 1907, it was sitting on American grocery store shelves, just in time for Prohibition.

During those years of forced temperance, sales of ginger ale topped all other soft drinks, but not because it soothed upset tummies. Its spicy flavor covered up the horrible taste of bootleg whiskey and bathtub gin, making it the most common ingredient added to illegal cocktails.

TUMMY TROUBLES

Throughout history and across cultures, ginger has been used to treat nausea and vomiting. The Greek physician Dioscorides (40–90 CE) wrote in his medical encyclopedia that ginger "gently stimulates the gut and is profitable for the stomach." The rhizome contains gingerols that slow down stomach contractions and reduce acids. Many medical studies support the use of ginger to treat an upset stomach. But—and this is a big BUT—most of the top brands of ginger ales on the market today don't contain enough actual ginger to do any good.

However, soothing upset tummies is exactly why ginger ale became king of the sky. In the early days of commercial air travel in the 1920s and 1930s, planes flew at lower altitudes with a lot more turbulence and noise than modern jets. Until the 1950s, the planes' cabins weren't pressurized or the air purified. Not only was cigarette smoking allowed on flights, but most people did it. Between the thick clouds of cigarette smoke and the horribly bumpy ride, there were a lot of queasy passengers. Flight attendants served ginger ale as a barf preventive.

Even after airplanes became pressurized and the air quality improved, the association between flying and ginger ale was set in peoples' minds. While not even in the top ten of most popular soft drinks on the ground, ginger ale rules in the air.

THE HIGHER THE BETTER

Some passengers order ginger ale on airplanes, not because they're feeling sick, but because it seems to taste better than normal. They're not imagining that. The air inside a plane is thin and dry, which dulls our taste buds, affecting sweet and salty the most. It's one reason airplane food seems bland. With ginger ale, the sugar is muted, but its delightful tangy flavor tickles our taste buds in a tantalizing way.

Natural herbalists claim numerous health benefits of ginger, sarsaparilla, and sassafras (once the safrole has been removed). Of the three, ginger has been clinically tested most often, with some evidence that it helps reduce inflammation and relieve nausea. It also has high amounts of antioxidants, which are believed to help reduce the risk of cancer. The few studies that tested sarsaparilla and sassafras show mixed results, but there are some indications that they may help with psoriasis and arthritis. Back in the good old days when root beer and ginger ale were actually made with pure plant extracts, these drinks might have been beneficial. However, today's soft drinks are usually artificially flavored, with little of the natural plant in them, plus they have added sugar. They're fun, fizzy, and flavorful, but not healthy.

TOP IT OFF

- March 13 is National Ginger Ale Day and August 6 is National Root Beer Day.
- Schweppes is the oldest existing soft drink brand starting in 1783. They introduced their ginger ale in 1870.
- When Barq's Root Beer hit the market in 1898, they didn't use the words "root beer" on their bottles to avoid being sued by Hires.
- Ginger ale is a nonalcoholic carbonated water that is sweetened and flavored with ginger and sugar. However, ginger beer has been fermented and brewed, creating a slight amount of alcohol. It's still considered nonalcoholic because at 0.5 percent, the level is below the standards of the FDA. Ginger beer has a much stronger flavor than ginger ale and is cloudy instead of clear.
- The largest sassafras tree in the world is in Owensboro, Kentucky. It's estimated to be 300 years old and stands twice the average height at over 100 feet tall.

⁑ Concoction Corner ⁂

Want to try a ginger ale with actual ginger in it? You can make your own like people used to do in the 1800s. This recipe is from *Dr. Chase's Recipes: or, Information for Everybody: An Invaluable Collection of About Eight Hundred Practical Recipes* by Dr. A. W. Chase, published in 1870. Don't be intimidated by the odd terms. A gill is an old measurement that equals one-half cup of fluid. Bruising ginger is fun! Wrap your ginger root in plastic wrap and then whack it with a wooden mallet until it's almost flat. That releases more of the juices and flavor. If you can't find lemon essence or extract, simply substitute two tablespoons of more lemon juice. Because this recipe doesn't use brewer's yeast for fermentation, this is a nonalcoholic blend.

YOU'LL NEED:

- 5 pounds white sugar
- 1 gill lemon juice
- ¼ pound honey
- 5 ounces ginger, bruised
- 4½ gallons water

Boil the ginger thirty minutes in three quarts of water, then add the other ingredients and strain. When cold, put in the white of an egg, well beaten, with one teaspoon of lemon essence—let stand for four days and bottle. It will keep for months—much longer than if yeast was used; the honey, however, operates mildly in place of yeast.

Chapter Seven

COLA WARS

OUT OF LITERALLY THOUSANDS OF SOFT DRINKS THAT HAVE existed at one time or another, Coca-Cola and Pepsi-Cola have survived and thrived. They were originally sold as tonics that promised relief from headaches, indigestion, and fatigue, but they dropped their medicinal claims in the early 1900s and have been battling each other for the top of the refreshment chart ever since. Their competition has been called the "cola wars," and it all began in a drugstore in Atlanta, Georgia, in 1886.

When pharmacist Dr. John Pemberton invented the first cola, he hoped it would sell a lot. He had already created perfumes, cough syrups, and liver pills, but none had made him rich. Pemberton thought he was going to rake in the dough with his French Wine Coca, a health tonic made with wine and the exotic new coca plant from Peru. But then the city of Atlanta doomed his drink when it banned alcohol.

Pemberton went back to his lab, removed the wine from the formula, and added the extract from another newly discovered plant, the West African kola nut. To cover up the kola's bitter taste, he dumped in a bunch of sugar.

Pemberton's new headache remedy and fatigue-fighting formula needed a name. Alliterative names were common at the time, such as Dr. Pierce's

Pleasant Purgative Pellets, Botanic Blood Balm, and Copeland's Cholera Cure. Pemberton's business partner, Frank Robinson, suggested combining the two plants' names into the catchy-sounding Coca-Cola. It was trademarked in 1887.

After a major advertising blitz, including newspaper ads and coupons for free samples, sales for Coca-Cola went up and up. Pemberton finally had a winner! Tragically, he didn't live long enough to see his cola become the king of all soft drinks. He died of stomach cancer in 1888.

THE DANGEROUS COCA PLANT

Since ancient times, Peruvians have chewed on the leaves of *Erythroxylum coca* as a stimulant. In 1860, German chemist Albert Niemann isolated the alkaloid cocaine from the leaves. In the beginning, the medical community prescribed this exciting new medicine for pain relief, indigestion, and, ironically, morphine addiction. When doctors realized that cocaine was as addictive and dangerous as morphine, it was banned in 1914. Even though the Coca-Cola Company didn't use pure cocaine, only a small amount of a less potent extract, it removed coca from the formula in 1903 due to safety concerns.

Frank Robinson brought the up-and-coming new beverage to Asa Candler, another Atlanta patent-medicine maker. Candler bought the rights to the formula and formed the Coca-Cola Company in 1892. Sales for Coca-Cola

kept climbing, and its success inspired copycats. To make it harder for imitators, the company had a bottle-design contest in 1915. They wanted a bottle so unique that everyone would know that it contained the real deal.

The Root Glass Company of Terre Haute, Indiana, took the challenge. One of their designers went to the library to find pictures of the cola nut for inspiration. Instead, he found pictures of the cocoa pod, which is used for making chocolate. Without knowing they had the wrong plant, they created a bottle shaped like the cocoa pod with the Coca-Cola script in a band across the middle. Candler loved it, even if it was the wrong bean. It worked because that iconic bottle is known around the world.

The Other Cola

Meanwhile, over in New Bern, North Carolina, pharmacist Caleb Bradham had developed his cola tonic in 1894. At the time, people ate too much meat and too few vegetables, which upset their stomachs. Bradham combined the kola nut with pepsin, an enzyme that helps digestion.

At first, he called it Brad's Drink and sold it in his pharmacy, but the positive response he got from customers encouraged him to dream bigger. He renamed it Pepsi-Cola in 1898 and started marketing it. Bradham's cola took off. He had to build a new plant in 1907 to keep up with orders. In a few years, there were 280 bottling plants in twenty-four states. Business was sweet until World War I sugar prices soured the company's finances. Bradham was forced to declare bankruptcy in 1923.

Roy Megargel acquired the trademark and reopened the Pepsi-Cola company in Virginia. He did okay for a few years until the stock market crash of 1929, when he had to sell the business before it went bankrupt again.

THE REAL KOLA

Native to West Africa, the *Cola acuminata* tree produces two-inch-long green pods with seeds inside. Those seeds are the kola nuts, which have caffeine like cacao beans and coffee beans. Local people chew the beans for energy and stamina. In the past, the cola companies used caffeine extracted from the kola nut until the cheaper artificial caffeine became available. Today, there is no longer any kola in colas.

✳✳ The Cola Wars Begin ✳✳

The next owner was Charles Guth, the president of the Loft chain of candy stores in New York. He bought Pepsi in 1931 because he was mad at Coke. His chain of two hundred soda fountains sold a lot of Coca-Cola, and he felt like he deserved a discount, but the Coke executives refused. So, Guth bought Pepsi-Cola, kicked Coke out of his stores, and replaced it with Pepsi.

Coca-Cola sued Pepsi for using the word "cola," because Coke claimed it was trademarked. The lawyers went back and forth for years. The courts finally decided that the word "cola" was an ingredient and couldn't be trademarked, so Pepsi got to keep its name.

In 1932, Guth went on the offensive again by selling Pepsi for a nickel in twelve-ounce bottles. Coca-Cola's bottles cost a nickel too, but they were half the size. Pepsi became "a nickel drink that's worth a dime." The ploy worked really well because the Great Depression had created a nation of penny-pinchers who liked a bargain.

Although Coke had the top spot, Pepsi was catching up. Unfortunately, Pepsi's gains didn't last long because a real war was coming.

✳✳ Colas on the Battleground ✳✳

Not long after the attack on Pearl Harbor, Robert Woodruff, the president of Coca-Cola, announced, "We will see that every man in uniform gets a bottle of Coca-Cola for five cents, wherever he is and whatever it costs our company." This extraordinary statement came true.

Coca-Cola got an exemption from the sugar rations to make products for the military. They planned to ship bottles of cola overseas, but the transports were full of weapons, ammunition, and troops and didn't have room for bulky pallets of heavy soft drink bottles. However, the syrup concentrate didn't

take up as much space. So, they sent the bottling equipment to the military bases and began making sodas on-site. The employees who went overseas to set up the bottling plants were nicknamed the "Coca-Cola Colonels."

Wherever the troops went, the Coca-Cola Colonels went too. They devised portable soda fountains that could be disassembled and reassembled as they moved with the troops. They even designed special fountains to fit on submarines. Whatever they had to do to produce colas, they did. By the end of the war, there were sixty-four bottling plants on every continent except Antarctica, and ten billion Cokes had been served.

For the homesick soldiers, airmen, marines, and seamen, getting an ice-cold Coca-Cola was like a hug from home. They cherished their sodas so much that an underground market developed to sell the precious product.

If a soldier wanted to, he could get anywhere from $5 to $40 for his allotted bottle. Prices went ridiculously high at some auctions, with one bottle selling for $4,000 in Italy.

While Coke secured the loyalty of the military people, poor Pepsi was stuck back in the states trying to get enough sugar to keep production going. A lot of soft drink companies went out of business during the war. Pepsi managed to find enough sweeteners to stay open. They took advantage of the fact that Coca-Cola was overseas and had special promotions to attract new customers at home. That helped a little, but they still lost ground in the popularity contest. The *American Legion Magazine* did a poll after the war, and 63 percent of respondents named Coca-Cola as their favorite soft drink while fewer than 8 percent said Pepsi. Clearly Coca-Cola had won that battle.

WWII SUGAR RATIONING

Before World War II, the United States imported most of its sugar from the Philippines, but when Japan captured the Philippines, those imports stopped. Sugar was the first item to be rationed at the beginning of the war, and the last to be restored. To keep this from happening again, the US government encouraged domestic sugar production, and now eleven states produce sugar beets and three states grow sugar cane. The USA is the fifth largest producer of sugar in the world and imports only approximately 15 percent of national sugar supplies.

No More Nickels

Since the first day Coca-Cola went on sale in 1886, the price had been five cents. Likewise, Pepsi-Cola had been charging five cents for its twelve-ounce bottle since its beginning. However, the cost of ingredients, bottles, labor, and shipping had gone up over the decades, and the companies couldn't make a profit anymore. Pepsi finally gave in to inflation and upped their price to ten cents in 1947.

The Coca-Cola Company also needed to charge more. They wanted to go up to no more than six or seven cents, but they had a real dilemma with their vending machines. Coke's machines only accepted nickels. You couldn't put a dime or quarter in and get change—only nickels. The company didn't want to charge a dime because they would lose their price advantage over Pepsi. In 1951, they actually had the nerve to ask Congress to issue a new coin worth seven and a half cents just for their vending machines. Of course Congress refused such a silly request.

It didn't really matter because Coca-Cola would be reconfiguring their vending machines soon anyway because cans were coming.

No Deposit, No Return

Soft drink companies still struggled to make a profit and they needed to reduce their costs. They thought that ditching glass bottles might help. Not only were the bottles expensive to make, but the deposit-refund system required that the empties be picked up from stores and sterilized, which was labor intensive.

Clicquot Club was the first soft drink company to try tin cans with their ginger ale in 1938, but the cans caused a yucky metallic taste. Then World War II happened and all metal went to the war effort. The beverage industry would have to wait until after the war to try cans again. Pepsi and Coke test-marketed tin cans, but the king of canned drinks became Royal Crown Cola, now known as RC Cola. By 1960, RC was the top seller in canned drinks. Its success spurred Coca-Cola and Pepsi to catch up.

ULTRA-USEFUL ALUMINUM

This versatile metal is used in cans, foils, kitchen utensils, and airplane parts. It's number thirteen on the periodic table with the symbol Al. Discovered in 1825 by Danish chemist Hans Oersted, aluminum is the third most common element in Earth's crust. Because of its tendency to bind with other elements, it was extremely difficult to obtain pure aluminum. In 1886, two men, Charles Hall in America and Paul Héroult in France, both twenty-two years old, discovered the same method to extract aluminum from ores using electricity. They didn't know about each other until they applied for patents. They became friends and shared the credit. The Hall-Héroult method is still used today. Coincidentally, they both died in 1914 at the age of fifty-one.

Then aluminum came to the canning business. RC Cola jumped on the new material in 1964, and Coke and Pepsi followed a couple of years later. Lightweight, unbreakable, and easy to stack, aluminum cans were ideal for vending machines, and by the late 1960s, almost all vending machines had them.

⚹ The Pepsi Challenge Pays Off *⚹*

In 1975, Pepsi set up tables in shopping malls, parks, and downtown city streets and asked random people to taste unmarked cola samples and pick the one they liked best. Then they aired commercials showing Coke fans being surprised to learn they had picked Pepsi. The "Take the Pepsi Challenge" campaign worked so well that by 1977, Pepsi outsold Coca-Cola in grocery stores.

Desperate to win back customers, Coca-Cola shocked the world by changing its formula and introducing New Coke on April 23, 1985. Coke's die-hard fans were furious! The company received forty thousand calls and letters of complaint. One irate customer said, "Changing Coke is just like breaking the American dream, like not selling hot dogs at a ball game."

The company realized that they'd made a big mistake. On July 10, 1985, they announced that Coca-Cola Classic would return. It was such a big deal that Peter Jennings of ABC interrupted a television show with a Breaking News alert. That day Coca-Cola's headquarters received eighteen thousand calls thanking them for bringing the old Coke back. New Coke never did sell very well and was discontinued in 2002.

Coke fans were so excited to have their beloved beverage back that sales shot through the roof. What seemed like the biggest marketing failure in the history of American business ended up winning Coca-Cola Classic the top spot.

For now, Coca-Cola is ahead in worldwide sales, but Pepsi is not far behind, and there are sure to be more battles in the cola wars.

OH NO! NUTRITION

It's hard to beat a refreshing gulp of an ice-cold cola. The syrupy sweetness with a bite of carbonation and a kick of caffeine makes colas truly delightful. Unfortunately, there's no nutritional value in them. They're basically flavored sugar water. If we were hummingbirds, colas might be a necessary part of our daily diet, but we're not hummingbirds. The average American consumes more sugar than is recommended, and some of that extra sugar comes from sweetened soft drinks.

TOP IT OFF

- Coca-Cola has so many different types of beverages that if you tried one a day, it would take you eleven years to taste them all.
- Pepsi set the record for the most expensive soft drink commercial during Super Bowl XXXVI on February 3, 2002. The commercial featured Britney Spears and cost $8.1 million, or $90,000 per second.
- Coca-Cola was the first soft drink to be drunk in space on the 1985 Space Shuttle Challenger.
- The first soft drink company to conduct public blind taste tests was Royal Crown Cola in 1940. They asked random people in hotel lobbies and train stations to taste several colas. RC Cola usually won.
- After the word "okay," "Coca-Cola" is the most recognized word on the planet.

✳✳ Concoction Corner ✳✳

Are your pennies looking dirty and dull? It's super easy to get them bright and shiny again. Over time, the copper coating on pennies binds with the oxygen in the air and changes color from bright orange to a dull brown. Most colas have phosphoric acid in them that eats that layer of copper and oxygen away, revealing a fresh layer of copper underneath.

COLA CLEANSER

YOU'LL NEED:

- Dirty pennies—pennies made before 1982 have more copper in them and will work better
- Disposable plastic cup
- Dark cola

Pour some cola in the cup and drop the pennies in. Let them sit overnight, and in the morning, you will have bright, shiny new pennies. DO NOT DRINK THE COLA! It will have copper in it, and copper is poisonous! Throw the cup away too.

Chapter Eight

SQUEEZED!

NEXT TIME YOU'RE IN THE GROCERY STORE, WALK DOWN THE juice aisle. Fancy some organic apple? How about white grape? Or would you prefer cranberry-pomegranate? If you'd been in a grocery store one hundred years ago, you'd be lucky to find grape juice. And if you wanted orange juice, you'd have to squeeze it yourself, if you could find an orange.

Fresh fruit juice is fragile. Unless it's refrigerated or pasteurized, it starts to spoil almost immediately. Before refrigerators, people didn't drink much juice, with the exception of lemonade. This tangy, sweet drink has been refreshing people for thousands of years. Even the Egyptians enjoyed it.

In Paris, France, in the 1600s, street vendors known as *limonadiers* walked around the city selling lemonade from a barrel strapped to their backs. Historians believe those *limonadiers* saved lives during a plague epidemic in the 1670s. How?

First, it's important to know that a bacterium causes the plague. Fleas carry the bacteria and then spread it around when they hop from host to host. Rats tend to have fleas. Rats also tend to eat everything. *What does any of this have to do with lemonade?* Well! Lemon peels contain limonene and linalool, two chemicals that are known to kill fleas and are used in pet

shampoos. When the *limonadiers* made a batch of lemonade, they tossed the leftover peels into the gutters, where the rats found them. When the rats ate the peels, the peels killed the fleas, and dead fleas couldn't spread the disease. People all over France were dying in droves, except the Parisians. It might have been one of the only times in history that being a litterbug turned out to be a good thing.

Pink Tastes Better

From Paris, lemonade became a favorite all over Europe and eventually in America. Like they did with tea, Americans added ice. Then they added color.

In the mid-1800s, traveling circuses crisscrossed the country. Circus-goers oohed and aahed at the acts, ogled the oddities, and guzzled lemonade—

the normal yellow kind. The first pink lemonade happened either by accident or out of desperation. While there's debate about which story is true, everyone agrees that it happened at a circus.

Henry Allott claimed to have invented pink lemonade while working in a circus concession stand. He had just mixed up a new batch when he accidentally dropped a candied apple in the pot. The apple's red coating dissolved into the liquid, turning it a lovely shade of pink. Staying true to the circus motto that "the show must go on," he sold it that way to the customers' delight.

That version sounds yummy, but Pete Conklin's story doesn't. Pete had sold out of lemonade and needed to make more, but he couldn't find any water. He saw a bucket of water near the trapeze lady's tent and grabbed it. When he started to pour in the sugar, he noticed a pair of red tights were soaking in it. Desperate, he scooped out the tights and made the lemonade in the pink-tinted water. Then he labeled it as a new "strawberry lemonade" and sold it all in less than an hour. Regardless of how it started, by the 1870s, pink lemonade was a circus standard.

Orange You Glad?

Lemonade wasn't the only exciting citrus. Originally from Asia and India, oranges became a sought-after delicacy in Europe in the 1600s. Spanish explorers took advantage of Florida's perfect climate to plant the first orange trees in the late 1500s. Later Spanish missionaries established Southern California's orange groves in 1700.

THE ORIGINS OF ORANGES

Citrus fruits have been around for eight million years and originated in the foothills of the Himalayas. All citrus fruits that we have today came from three ancestors: mandarin (*Citrus reticulata*), pomelo (*Citrus maxima*), and citron (*Citrus medica*). It's believed that lemons are the result of a cross between lime, citron, and pomelo. Sweet oranges, such as navel and Valencia, came from pomelos and mandarins. The English word "orange" is from the French word for gold, *or*.

Americans have had oranges for more than three hundred years, but we didn't get orange juice in our grocery stores until the 1950s. What took so long? First, citrus farmers had to figure out how to get oranges from the coasts of California and Florida to the rest of the country before they rotted. They also had to learn how to stop the juice from fermenting. And then they had to convince consumers that OJ was an important part of a healthy diet.

✳✳ All Aboard! ✳✳

In the 1800s, oranges were such a rare and exotic fruit for most people in the United States that children might see them only once a year in their Christmas stocking. Some Americans went their whole lives without ever tasting a fresh orange.

Florida growers had an advantage over California with their location on the East Coast, but it was still a challenge to keep the fruit from shriveling up before it reached customers. There was no way California oranges could survive the six-month trip across the continent to markets on the East Coast.

That all changed with the opening of the Transcontinental Railroad in 1869 and the development of ice-bunker train cars. The California Fruit Growers Exchange (which became Sunkist) could ship their fruit to the rest of the country in the chilled compartments. The ice-bunker cars also helped the Florida Citrus Exchange.

With the transportation problem solved and orange production at an all-time high, West Coast and Florida orange growers needed to find a way to use all their fruit. One idea was to turn it into juice. In the 1920s, they tried canning fresh juice, but the acids reacted with the lining of the tin cans, making it taste like cleaning fluid.

The citrus industry struggled with a viable way to sell juice and didn't get a break until World War II. The United States military needed a way to provide vitamin C to the troops. In 1942, scientists gathered at the

United States Department of Agriculture's Citrus Products Station in Winter Haven, Florida, to create a preservable, transportable citrus drink for the military.

CONNECTING THE COUNTRY

With the Pacific Railway Act of 1862, President Abraham Lincoln challenged two rail companies to connect the West Coast to the rest of America. The Central Pacific Railroad started in Sacramento, California, and the Union Pacific started in Omaha, Nebraska. The final spike was hammered in on May 10, 1869, in Promontory, Utah. The Transcontinental Railroad cut the travel time between the East Coast and the West Coast from six months to less than one week.

In 1948, they finally developed a method of condensing the juice first and then freezing it so that it didn't destroy the vitamins and still tasted decent. That was too late to help with the war, but not too late for grocery stores. Compared to squeezing oranges, shoppers liked the ease of dumping a can of frozen concentrate into a pitcher and stirring in water.

The citrus industry spent massive amounts of advertising dollars convincing the public that vitamin C was vital to overall health and that drinking orange juice was the best way to get it. OJ had to compete against the cheaper fruit-flavored products enriched with vitamin C, such as Hi-C and Tang, but sales did improve.

Eventually, production techniques and packaging innovations made it possible to sell ready-to-serve orange juice in grocery stores. Once people discovered what fresh OJ tasted like, frozen concentrate sales dropped. By 1985, ready-to-serve bottles outsold frozen concentrate.

ASCORBIC ACID

Ascorbic acid, also known as vitamin C, promotes the growth and health of our bones, teeth, gums, blood vessels, and ligaments. It also helps our major organs function properly. Unlike most animals, humans don't make their own vitamin C. We have to get it from our food. Scurvy is caused by vitamin C deficiency and was common among sailors and soldiers who didn't eat enough fruits or vegetables. Symptoms of scurvy include bleeding gums, loose teeth, and bleeding under the skin. Left untreated, it can lead to death. As early as the 1750s, doctors believed citrus fruit helped prevent scurvy, but they didn't know why. That question was finally answered in 1930, when Hungarian scientist Albert Szent-Györgyi isolated ascorbic acid in a series of experiments with guinea pigs. He used guinea pigs because they can't produce their own vitamin C, either, like humans.

Tasty Temperance Juices

Unlike oranges that were mainly grown to be eaten, apples and grapes were more prized for their juices, or at least what could be made from their juice.

For over eight thousand years, humans have been turning grape juice into wine, and for about two thousand years, they've been turning apple juice into hard cider. It took the temperance movement and pasteurization to switch these juices into healthy, nonalcoholic drinks.

FERMENTATION

When bacteria, yeast, or molds get into foods or liquids, they use their enzymes to break down the food's sugars into simpler compounds. Sometimes the results are good, like yogurt, cheese, and bread. But other times, it ruins the food, like soured milk. When yeast is added to fruit juices, it breaks down the juices' natural sugars into alcohol and carbon dioxide, turning grapes into wine and apples into cider.

Dr. Thomas Bramwell Welch was a dentist and a Methodist minister who hated alcohol. It really bothered him that his church served real wine at communion. In 1869, he devised a way to pasteurize Concord grape juice to stop the fermentation process so it would be alcohol-free. He called it Dr. Welch's Unfermented Wine. He gave it to his congregation and sold it to other churches as well.

Welch's son, Charles Welch, was also a dentist, but he was more interested in his dad's juice business than teeth. Charles saw the potential of marketing grape juice as a family-friendly health tonic and not just as a wine substitute. In 1875, he changed the name to Welch's Grape Juice.

Thomas didn't like his son's fanciful business ideas and wrote him a letter saying, "The interest you have in grape juice is not worth half as much as your interest in dentistry. As a dentist you can make much more than with grape juice." Charles didn't listen to him. Instead, he closed his dental practice to concentrate on growing the beverage business.

Charles advertised in magazines and medical journals touting the health benefits of Welch's Grape Juice. He also set up a booth at the Chicago World's Fair in 1893 and gave out samples. That international introduction, plus his savvy advertising, pushed sales so much that for a time, he ran out of Concord grapes. In 1897, he moved the growing company to Westfield, New York, because he needed a bigger production facility. It seems that Charles made the right decision to quit dentistry.

✳✳ An Apple a Day ✳✳

When Prohibition loomed, cider makers scrambled to learn how to make plain apple juice. It was going to be a big adjustment because cider had been a part of daily American life since colonial times. When the English and

Dutch colonized America in the 1600s, they brought apple seeds with them to establish groves as quickly as possible so they could make cider. Back then, you'd be hard-pressed to find someone who didn't drink several pints a day, even children.

Cider makers figured out how to pasteurize the juice to stop fermentation, but that wasn't their only challenge. They also had to convince the Prohibition committees that their apple juice wouldn't be made into cider later. In 1922, the Hildick Apple Juice Company and Duffy-Mott had to sue to get their licenses approved.

It took a while, but apple juice slowly gained fans, mostly among children. After pediatricians began recommending it for babies and toddlers in the 1950s, it became America's number one juice according to most surveys. Other surveys give the top spot to orange juice.

MALUS DOMESTICA—THE APPLE

According to DNA analysis, the first apples (*Malus sieversii*) came from the mountains of Kazakhstan around fifty million years ago. This fruit is known as an "extreme heterozygote" because it can inherit a wide variety of traits from its parents. Apples contain 57,000 genes, almost double the 30,000 in humans. There are 7,500 varieties of apples in the world. Although there are more than 2,500 varieties in the United States, only 100 are grown commercially. To reproduce favorite varieties, farmers graft the desired type onto the rootstock of another tree.

✳✳ Lunch Box Bonanza ✳✳

When Swedish businessman Ruben Rausing came up with the idea for a new container for milk in 1963, he had no idea that he would also revolutionize the juice industry in America. He wanted to create milk packaging that didn't require refrigeration because European fridges were very small. He thought it would make everyone's life easier if the milk could be stored in the pantry. It took him a few years, but he finally invented the Tetra Brik. He also developed a method to seal it under completely sterile conditions so that no bacteria could get in the beverage and spoil it.

In the United States, the dairy industry didn't see any advantage to investing in new packaging when Americans had plenty of room in their big fridges for milk. However, the juice industry got very excited. The new beverage container would fit perfectly in children's lunch boxes. The Apple & Eve company became one of the first to adopt the Tetra Brik in 1982, and other companies soon followed. By 1986, 20 percent of all juice sales came in boxes. Since they were introduced in America, more than four billion juice boxes have been sold.

Nowadays, in the juice department, you can choose from boxes, bottles, cans, jars, fresh-squeezed, concentrated, and frozen, and that doesn't include the hundreds of flavors. Juices have evolved from an occasional treat to a common, everyday product in the last century with probably more innovations to come.

OH NO! NUTRITION

The health benefits from fruit juices are undeniable. Besides containing important vitamins and minerals, fruit juices also have antioxidants that have been shown to lower the risk of cancer. The *2020–2025 Dietary Guidelines for Americans* recommends that juices should be 100 percent juice with no added sugars. It also recommends that whenever possible, it's better to *eat* the fruit rather than *drink* its juice. The whole fruit includes more fiber and vitamins than juice.

TOP IT OFF

- There really are pink lemons! The variegated Eureka lemon looks like a miniature watermelon on the outside and has pink pulp inside. It gets its color from a high concentration of lycopene, just like pink grapefruit. Unfortunately, the juice runs clear instead of pink.
- In 1877, First Lady Lucy Hayes, wife of the nineteenth president of the United States, Rutherford B. Hayes, banned alcohol from being served in the White House, earning her the nickname "Lemonade Lucy."
- It took Ephraim Wales Bull many years and more than 22,000 grape species to finally produce what he believed was the perfect grape in 1849. He named it after his hometown, Concord, Massachusetts. The Concord grape became the basis of Welch's Grape Juice.
- The United States Department of Agriculture has an apple collection in Geneva, New York, with 2,937 different varieties.

⁎⁎ Concoction Corner ⁎⁎

Acids such as lemon juice and vinegar have more hydrogen than bases such as baking soda or soap. Water is neutral. The pH scale goes from 0 (very acidic) to 14 (very basic). Red grape juice can act as an indicator and will change colors in the presence of an acid or a base.

GRAPE JUICE ACID INDICATOR

YOU'LL NEED:

- Coffee filter
- 100 percent red grape juice with no additives
- Water
- Mixing bowl
- Cotton swabs
- Several liquids to test, such as vinegar, water, baking soda, milk, soap

Make the test pH strip by soaking the coffee filter in grape juice for at least 10 minutes. Let it dry and then cut the paper into strips.

Dip a cotton swab into one of the liquids and wipe it on the test strip. Use a new swab and a new test strip for each liquid.

Acids will turn the grape juice test strips pink while bases will turn either blue or green.

Chapter Nine

PACKETS AND POUCHES OF PUNCHES

ALTHOUGH WE THINK OF FRUIT PUNCHES AS A KIDS' DRINK, the first punches were substitutes for bad beer. When English sailors traveled to India in the early 1600s, their beer spoiled in the tropical heat. Doing without alcohol was simply not an option! They were sailors, after all. They tried the local liquor, but it tasted horrible to them. So, they poured it in a big bucket and mixed in fruit juices and spices. Then they took turns dipping their mugs in it.

The word "punch" is believed to come from the Hindi word *panj* for five because of the basic ingredients in the old recipes. A commonly used phrase was "one sour, two sweet, three strong, four weak, and spices make five" referring to the ingredients: citrus, sugar, alcohol, water, and spice.

The sailors brought their boozy bucket back to England. Over several generations, that bucket morphed into ornate silver punch bowls that were

the highlight of fancy parties and holiday celebrations. Those expensive punch bowls became status symbols of wealth and refinement.

SOCIAL SILVER

In English high society, where silver equaled status, all the top snobs had ornate punch bowls. American silversmiths carried on that tradition by creating beautiful silver punch bowls for wealthy colonists. Once such punch bowl, made by New York silversmith Cornelius Kierstede between 1700 and 1710, sold at an auction for $5.9 million in 2010. Paul Revere Jr. crafted one of the most famous silver punch bowls in American history in 1768. It honors the Massachusetts representatives known as the Glorious Ninety-Two, who were instrumental in the Revolutionary War. The Sons of Liberty Bowl is in the Museum of Fine Arts in Boston.

Americans loved punch, too, but then Prohibition took the kick out of it. With the alcohol left out, it became kid-friendly and a kid favorite. No one had really thought about making a beverage for kids before this, but fruit punches gave Edwin Perkins an idea.

✳✳ Too Kool! ✳✳

Perkins grew up helping in his parents' general store in Nebraska. He understood the retail business and thought he could make more money if he made his own products and sold them directly to the public. He founded the Perkins Products Company, which offered over one hundred items, such as medicines, tonics, and perfumes. He also printed the labels and catalogs on his own printing press.

One of his most successful products was a bottled drink concentrate called Fruit Smack. Although sales were good, he had problems with the bottles breaking in shipment. Inspired by packages of Jell-O, he dehydrated his Fruit Smack into a powder and printed paper packages on his printing press. In 1928, he introduced Kool-Ade in six flavors: grape, lemon-lime, cherry, orange, raspberry, and strawberry.

Across the country, newspaper ads announced, "Kool-Ade Soft Drink Flavors. Just use a package of Kool-Ade, add sugar and cold water and you have 10 glasses of delicious and refreshing soft drink. 10 c per package." For moms on a budget, this was a no-brainer. They couldn't even get one bottle of Canada Dry Ginger Ale for ten cents! And Kool-Ade came in bright red, orange, green, and purple. What kid wouldn't want a purple tongue or a green mustache? It didn't take long for Kool-Ade to become kids' favorite drink in the 1930s.

FOOD COLORINGS

Before the 1906 Pure Food and Drugs Act, anyone could put anything into foods and drinks. For example, chalk was added to milk to make it whiter. When Kool-Ade entered the market in 1929, there were fifteen FDA approved food colorings, of which six are still in use today. Many drink manufacturers prefer using artificial dyes because they're cheaper and last longer than natural colorings. Most natural food dyes are plant-based, such as the orangey carotenoids (carrots, pumpkins), the greenish chlorophylls (alfalfa), and the bluesy anthocyanins (grapes, blueberries). But one, the reddish carminic, is made from crushing the cochineal insect. Have you been eating bugs? Check labels for carmine, carminic acid, cochineal, or Natural Red 4.

During the Great Depression, Kool-Ade dropped its price from a reasonable ten cents to an even better five cents. It also changed the name from "Kool-Ade" to "Kool-Aid." The FDA expected beverages with "ade" in their name to be made of fruit, and Kool-Aid certainly didn't fit that description.

In 1954, Kool-Aid's newspaper ads started featuring a smiling pitcher as a mascot. Kool-Aid Man came alive in a 1975 television commercial when he burst through a wall in a bowling alley to save sweaty kids from thirst. The Kool-Aid Man became so popular that he got his own video game and comic books.

Although Kool-Aid was one of the first beverages to be marketed to children, it wasn't the last.

Competition with a Capital "C"

After World War II's sugar shortages finally ended, new beverages sprouted on the market like weeds after a spring rain, and the kids' market got competitive. The citrus industry was in an all-out advertising push to have OJ as a part of every American breakfast. To make juice more convenient, they tried to sell it in tin cans. Unfortunately, the acids in the orange juice reacted with the metal, resulting in a tinny taste.

Niles A. Foster had a better idea. He came up with a beverage using 10 percent real fruit juice and supplemented it with vitamin C. Then he sorted out the issue with the tin cans so that his drink didn't taste metallic. He called it Hi-C because—OBVIOUSLY—it was high in vitamin C.

Foster also thought grocery stores and shoppers might be tired of the deposit-refund system on glass bottles and would be thrilled with throwaway cans. Grocery stores didn't like the empty bottles taking up warehouse space, and shoppers didn't like the inconvenience of rinsing and returning them.

In 1949, Foster introduced Hi-C Orange-Ade in grocery stores. The advertisements emphasized that Hi-C had the adult daily requirement of vitamin C and that it came in sterilized cans that didn't need refrigeration. The ads also included lines like "no deposit, no bottles to return." Although those claims were true, the ads also said that Hi-C was made from luscious, tree-ripened oranges without admitting that only 10 percent of the drink was real fruit juice.

Foster obviously knew what consumers cared about, because in less than five years, Hi-C became the top-selling canned beverage on grocery store shelves. That success attracted corporate attention, and the Minute Maid company bought the brand in 1954.

DEPOSIT-REFUND SYSTEM

In the late 1800s and through World War II, it was cheaper for beverage companies to reuse bottles than to make new ones. With the deposit-refund system, shoppers paid an extra five cents for their drink, and when they returned the rinsed bottle to the store, they got a nickel back. When cans became available in the 1950s, fewer glass bottles were used, and the deposit-refund systems fell by the wayside. However, the method is successful in encouraging recycling, and ten states currently use it. Three of the states, Oregon, Michigan, and Maine, have return rates of over 80 percent.

Minute Maid took Hi-C promotions to new heights in 1956. After Hawaii schoolchildren had sent in enough Hi-C labels, Minute Maid donated two giraffes, Hi-Cecil and Hi-Cecilia, to the Honolulu Zoo.

✳✳ Aloha ✳✳

From the success of Kool-Aid and Hi-C, beverage manufacturers realized that kid-friendly drinks made money. Reuben P. Hughes wanted in on those profits. In 1946, he bought a popular ice cream syrup called Leo's Hawaiian Punch and turned it into one of the top kids' drinks of its time.

The original Hawaiian Punch recipe was created by three friends, A. W. Leo, Tom Yates, and Ralph Harrison, in a garage in Fullerton, California, in 1934. They used fruits imported from Hawaii to make a tropical-flavored syrup that they sold to soda fountains and ice cream shops.

At some point, customers discovered that the syrup tasted great when mixed with water, but they could only get it at soda fountains, one glass at a time. That's when Hughes got involved. He bought the brand, made it into a drink, and started selling it in forty-six-ounce cans at grocery stores in 1950. Hi-C had some competition.

Advertising for Hawaiian Punch emphasized the five tropical fruits in the ingredients (orange, pineapple, guava, papaya, and passion fruit) but didn't mention that the drink contained only 10 percent of real fruit juice. Families fell for the tropical flavor, and by 1955, Hawaiian Punch was one of the top-selling fruit punches in the country.

 Blast Off

In 1957, General Foods introduced Tang, a new orange-flavored beverage powder enriched with vitamin C. Its newspaper ads claimed, "No Squeezing, No Unfreezing—Your Tang jar needs no refrigeration. Make as much as you want—a glass or a quart." Obviously, Tang wanted to steal some of the customers away from the new frozen orange juice concentrate.

Even with heavy advertising, Tang didn't fly off the shelves. Then in 1960, the National Aeronautics and Space Administration (NASA) needed a lightweight, vitamin-rich beverage that didn't need refrigeration and was easy to use inside the tight confines of a space capsule. Tang checked all the boxes.

ON A MISSION

NASA's Project Mercury was the first series of space flights with human astronauts (monkeys had been going up since 1948). The six flights between 1961 and 1963 helped NASA scientists prepare for landing a man on the moon. The first two flights went up into space and came right back down. The third flight, piloted by astronaut John Glenn, orbited the earth on February 20, 1962. NASA scientists wanted to test astronauts' ability to eat and drink in zero gravity, so even though Glenn's flight lasted only 4 hours and 55 minutes, he had a big picnic packed for him.

To solve the problem of how to mix the powder and water in zero gravity, NASA scientists created a sealed pouch of powder. The astronaut would insert a sharp tube, squirt the water inside, and shake it up. Then they pulled out the tube and replaced it with a straw.

Tang got its first chance to go into space on the Mercury 3 flight with John Glenn on February 20, 1962. For the next ten years, Tang quenched the astronauts' thirst in the Gemini and Apollo missions. General Foods took full advantage of the NASA association by airing television commercials bragging that Tang had been "chosen for the Gemini astronauts."

American children were over the moon excited about anything connected with space. If the astronauts drank Tang, they wanted it too. Sales sky-rocketed, and for a few years, Tang was everywhere and in everything. There were recipes for pies, cakes, cookies, gelatin desserts, punches, and teas made with Tang. Unfortunately, after the novelty of the space program wore off, Tang's sales splashed down in America. But not in the rest of the world. It's still very popular in South America and Asia.

The Pouch Pounces

Kool-Aid, Hi-C, and Hawaiian Punch were doing pretty well for themselves in the kids' market. They introduced new flavors from time to time to keep their customers interested, but those flavors were no match for the new idea that rocked the beverage world—fruit punch in a pouch.

Rudolf Wild, a German food manufacturer, believed in all-natural products and set out to make a fruit drink without chemicals. He wanted the container to be lighter and easier to pack than bottles or cartons, while also preserving the juices so that they didn't need refrigeration. Wild succeeded beyond his wildest dreams.

His Capri-Sonne (the original name) came out in Germany in 1969 in two-flavors, lemon and orange. For the next few years, it was only available in Europe. It didn't hit American stores until 1982, but when it did, it made a big impact. In only twelve years, Capri-Sun became the top children's drink in the United States, surpassing all the old favorites.

Kids loved poking the straw into the space-age foil pouch and squeezing the drink out. They also enjoyed blowing up the empty pouch and popping it.

Parents liked real fruit juices and no preservatives or artificial colors. And the light, portable, packable pouches were a ten out of ten on the convenience scale.

Punches have come a long way from sailors dipping their mugs into the big wooden buckets to the pouches of sweet fruitiness for kids. What will people come up with next?

HISTORY OF STRAWS

Humans have been using straws for over five thousand years, according to an archaeological discovery in 1897. Three-foot gold and silver tubes were dug up in Maykop, Russia, which were used to sip from a large, shared vessel. At other times in human history, reedy grasses and hollowed-out stalks of plants were used. In 1888, Marvin Stone invented the paper straw, to the delight of soda fountain fans. Plastic straws hit the scene in the 1960s, which seemed like a great idea at the time. Unfortunately, plastic is not good for the environment. Some estimates put the use of plastic straws at five hundred million a day. To address environmental concerns, some straws are being made of bamboo, silicone, metal, or PLA (polylactic acid, which is made of compostable corn resin). Of course, there still is the option of using good old paper.

Just as with soft drinks, fruit punches typically have more sugar than is good for us. Concerns have also been raised about some of the artificial colorings in them. Even though the food colorings are FDA approved, some people can have allergic reactions to them. Some of the fruity beverages are made with a small percentage of real fruit juice and have been fortified with vitamins. While that sounds more nutritious than soft drinks, they don't provide all the fiber, vitamins, and antioxidants that you would get if you ate real fruit (not to mention they're high in sugar). As with any sweet treat, read the label and make a wise choice about your daily sugar intake.

TOP IT OFF

- Fayis Nazer holds the Guinness World Record for the fastest time to drink a Capri-Sun. He did it in 11.86 milliseconds on January 29, 2022, in Abu Dhabi, United Arab Emirates.
- Hastings, Nebraska, celebrates its hometown legendary beverage each August with the Kool-Aid Days Festival. Kool-Aid is the official soft drink of Nebraska.
- Tang's original orange flavor is the worldwide top seller, but other flavors are popular too. The Chinese enjoy lemon, Brazilians like pineapple, Filipinos prefer mango, and Mexicans favor tamarind.
- After quenching kids' thirst for twenty-five years, Kool-Aid Man's footprints were eternalized at a ceremony at Mann's Chinese Theatre in Hollywood on May 11, 2000. His feet measured 15¼ inches long and 10¼ inches wide. The footprints are now in the Hastings Museum in Hastings, Nebraska.

✳✳ Concoction Corner ✳✳

There's no reason to wonder about artificial food colorings when you can make your own at home.

- **YELLOW:** Turmeric is a strong dye and will easily stain your clothes, so be careful with it. Boil ½ teaspoon of ground turmeric with ¼ cup water. Allow to cool before storing in an airtight class jar.

- **GREEN:** Boil one cup of fresh spinach for 5 minutes. Drain and place in a blender with 3 tablespoons of water. Filter out the solids, and the liquid left will be the dye.

- **BLUE:** Simmer shredded red cabbage for 10 minutes. The water will turn purple. Add baking soda, ½ teaspoon at a time, until you achieve the color you want.

- **RED:** This one is super easy: pomegranate juice.

To make all these more vibrant, make them more concentrated by simmering them in a pot to reduce the liquid.

Chapter Ten

GAME ON!

WE WOULDN'T HAVE SPORTS DRINKS TODAY IF IT WEREN'T for the ridiculous theory that athletes wouldn't be able to compete at their best if they drank water because it slowed them down. Since water is heavy, people thought less of it in their bodies meant they would be lighter and faster. In the early 1900s, athletes practiced "purposeful dehydration," and it almost killed Thomas Hicks, the winner of the 1904 Olympic marathon.

When Hicks and the other runners lined up for the start of the marathon on August 30, in St. Louis, Missouri, the heat index was ninety degrees Fahrenheit. The grueling course covered 24.85 miles on mostly dirt roads with seven hills.

THE RACE NAMED AFTER A TOWN

In 490 BCE, the Greek messenger Pheidippides ran from Marathon to Athens to share the news that the invading Persian army had been defeated. When he reached the Acropolis, he announced, "*Nike! Nike! Nenikekiam!*" (Victory! Victory! We have won!), then dropped dead. To honor Pheidippides at the first modern Olympics in 1896, a 25-mile race between Marathon and Athens was held. The distance was extended to 26.2 miles at the 1908 Olympic Games in London, England, supposedly because Queen Alexandra wanted the race to start on the lawn of Windsor Castle so the little royals could watch from their windows.

Hicks took an early lead, but he was struggling at the ten-mile marker. He begged his trainers for a drink. They refused. At mile seventeen, Hicks desperately pleaded for water, but his trainers gave him a shot of strychnine instead. That sounds unbelievable now, because strychnine is a deadly poison, but back then it was used in small doses to stimulate the muscles. It worked for a few miles, but then he began hallucinating. Instead of water, his trainers gave him egg whites and brandy. Plodding along in a delirious state, he entered the stadium for the final lap. He managed a final surge of energy to cross the finish line before collapsing.

After being declared the winner, doctors whisked Hicks away for emergency treatment, and he survived, barely. His time of 3:28:45 was the slowest winning time for an Olympic marathon ever. Out of the thirty-one runners who started, only fourteen finished.

Football Fever, Also Known as Heatstroke

Football coaches also believed in limiting fluids during games. The legendary Paul "Bear" Bryant, the University of Alabama football coach, never allowed water breaks during practices or games. A few soft-hearted coaches would let their players sip-swish-spit, but swallowing water was a no-no.

That was the norm until August 1965, when Dewayne Douglas, an assistant coach for the freshman football team at the University of Florida, questioned the wisdom of it. In one week, twenty-five of Douglas's players had been admitted to the hospital with heatstroke. To tackle this problem, he asked Dr. Robert Cade and Dr. Dana Shires, both University of Florida medical school professors and researchers, to come up with a way to keep his players on the field and out of the hospital.

You're probably thinking, "Why didn't they just drink water?" At the time, athletic trainers believed that it took too long for water to empty out of the stomach and might cause stomach cramps.

As a sports fan and a kidney specialist, Dr. Cade couldn't resist the challenge. He and Shires enlisted the help of two other doctors in the department, Alex de Quesada and Jim Free. If they were going to come up with a solution to replace sweat, first they needed to know what was in it. To capture the perspiration, freshman players, affectionately known as

"Baby Gators," wore long rubber gloves during practice. The sweat dripped down their arms and pooled in the gloves. Then the gloves were emptied into lab containers. The docs also took blood and urine samples from their test subjects before and after practice.

After analyzing the samples, Cade made the first batch of replacement fluid using water, glucose, and two electrolytes—sodium and potassium. Good idea, but extremely bad taste. It was so awful, Cade puked after trying it. There's no way the players would drink this stuff. The docs had to flavor it and finally settled on lemon juice. It still didn't taste good, but at least it didn't make anyone barf.

EXCELLENT ELECTROLYTES

Electrolytes are minerals in our body that help our nerves, muscles, brain, and heart function properly. They include sodium, calcium, potassium, chloride, phosphate, and magnesium. The concentration of the minerals in the blood is called the plasma osmolality. When we sweat, we lose fluid and electrolytes, which can change that concentration. If we get too dehydrated, the mineral levels may get so low that it affects the function of our nerves, heart, and muscles.

 The Field Test

Every season, the Baby Gators would play against the varsity B team in a game known as the Toilet Bowl. With more experience and more muscle, the

varsity team almost always won. On October 1, 1965, the varsity scored early and led at halftime, as expected. But the Baby Gators had a secret weapon—the doctors' solution. After drinking it, the Baby Gators came out in the second half as strong as the first and thoroughly thrashed the exhausted, dehydrated varsity.

This got the attention of the head coach, Ray Graves, but he still wasn't convinced that he should change training tactics. However, the team's head trainer, Jim Cunningham, *was* convinced. Without telling Coach Graves, Cunningham asked the doctors to bring their solution to the next game, which happened to be against the heavily favored Louisiana State University (LSU).

The doctors stayed up late into the night, squeezing lemon juice and mixing gallons of the solution. The next day, they were on the sidelines, handing out cups of it to the players. The Gators roared into the second half and beat LSU 14–7 in a big upset. That made Coach Graves a believer. He ordered enough solution for the rest of the season.

They couldn't keep calling it the Doctor's Solution. They tossed around a few names such as Cade's Cola and Cade's Ade, but Jim Free's suggestion of Gatorade won.

 Gatorade Gets the Glory

The Florida team used Gatorade for the rest of the 1965 season and the 1966 season. The doctors decided that putting ice in the coolers diluted the solution too much, so they started serving it in small milk cartons.

Neil Amdur, a sports reporter from the *Miami Herald*, noticed all the empty milk cartons on the sidelines and asked Dr. Cade if the players were drinking milk. Dr. Cade answered, "Every year, 20 to 50 boys die in this country from heat strokes while playing football. I wanted to do something to help eliminate this and we've designed an electrolyte solution that accurately replaces the fluids an athlete loses." This interview appeared in the paper on November 30, 1966. The secret of Gatorade was out.

TOO HOT TO TROT

Heatstroke is basically your body overheating. Symptoms include a core body temperature of 104 degrees Fahrenheit or above, confusion, slurred speech, nausea, headache, racing heart rate, low blood pressure, and flushed skin. Without immediate medical care, heatstroke can cause permanent damage to the brain and other organs, and it can be fatal. According to the Centers for Disease Control and Prevention, an average of seven hundred people die of heat-related causes a year.

✳✳ Gatorade Goes Pro ✳✳

The doctors thought Gatorade might have mass appeal, but they didn't have the resources to produce it on a big scale. After shopping it around, they sold the formula and rights to the Stokely-Van Camp company in May 1967 for $5,000 plus five cents on every gallon sold. Guess who became multimillionaires plus?

The first thing Stokely-Van Camp did was make Gatorade taste better. Their food chemist, June Davis, who had experience with Jell-O, worked with the formula to add more sugar in a way that didn't slow the absorption rate.

WHO WANTS TO BE A FOOD SCIENTIST?

Does coming up with a new flavor of Gatorade sound fun to you? Food scientists create products; invent packages; and develop freezing, frying, and filleting techniques. They analyze the vitamin and mineral content of foods and study how different processing methods affect taste and aroma. They use chemistry, engineering, and physics in an entirely fun-filled foodie way.

Famous for their pork and beans, Stokely-Van Camp knew all about canning, but their plan to can Gatorade didn't work out. The salty solution eroded the lining of the cans, causing leakage. Stokely tried glass bottles next, but coaches didn't like having breakable containers on the sidelines.

Then Stokely tried pouches of powdered concentrate. Worried that their customers might not like mixing their own batches of beverage, Stokely sweetened the deal with free coolers and cups, with the Gatorade logo on them, of course. That turned out to be a brilliant marketing move. Now every time fans watched a game, they saw sports stars drinking Gatorade.

✳✳ A New Tradition ✳✳

That free publicity was good, but a drop in the cooler compared to the Gatorade dunk. The very first one happened on October 28, 1984, after the New York Giants beat the Washington Redskins (now known as the Washington Commanders). In the week before the game, Giants coach Bill Parcells had been extra hard on nose guard Jim Burt in practices. When the clock ticked down to a Giants victory, Burt impulsively picked up a Gatorade cooler and dumped it on Parcells. Shocked teammates waited for Parcells to explode, but he shocked them again by bursting out in laughter. The coach got doused again after the next win. Obviously, Parcells could've stopped these freezing green showers, but he didn't want to jinx the team's winning streak. The Giants went on to win the Super Bowl that year, and the Gatorade dunk (also called the Gatorade bath and Gatorade shower) became a sports tradition.

Gatorade's success got the attention of Coca-Cola and PepsiCo, the biggest beverage companies in the world. They brought their own sports drinks to market. Pepsi started with Mountain Dew Sport in 1989, but later changed the name to All Sport. Coca-Cola came out with Powerade in 1990. Countless other companies sold sports drinks too. No more "purposeful dehydration" for this generation—Gatorade had started a hydration revolution.

✳✳ Not Just for Athletes ✳✳

The idea that sports drinks helped athletic performance opened up the possibility that drinks could help people achieve in other ways. Need more energy to finish that project before the deadline? Have a final exam to cram for? Have to work a double shift? No problem, have an energy drink. By combining a high amount of caffeine and sugar with vitamins, amino acids, and other natural substances, energy drinks claim to increase mental alertness, energy, and stamina. Unfortunately, they can also cause rapid heart rates, nervousness, and headaches.

BETTER WITH A BULL?

One of the most common ingredients in energy drinks is taurine, an amino acid first isolated from the bile of an ox in 1827. The name "taurine" came from the Latin word *taurus*, for bull. Although not conclusive, there are some studies that show taurine improves cardiovascular function and muscular endurance. Some people have speculated that it was added to Red Bull's formula just for its bullish name. Taurine is found naturally in our bodies and in many common foods, such as eggs, milk, chicken, fish, and meat. In a normal diet, adults will get around fifty to sixty milligrams of taurine a day. Energy drinks contain as much as two thousand milligrams. Researchers haven't determined yet if more is better.

Although not the first energy drink, Red Bull was the first internationally known brand and is credited with creating this drink category. It was invented in 1976 by Chaleo Yoovidhya in Thailand and sold there under the name Krating Daeng (which is "red bull" in Thai). When Austrian Dietrich Mateschitz traveled to Thailand in 1982, he tried a Krating Daeng, and it helped him get over his jet lag. The product excited him so much, he partnered with Yoovidhya to open the Red Bull GmbH company in Austria. To cater to European taste buds, Mateschitz modified the formula and added carbonation. On April 1, 1987, the first Red Bull went on sale.

In a unique marketing strategy, the Red Bull company sponsored extreme sports such as cliff diving, air races, and mountain bike competitions. The company even created a new wacky event called Flugtag ("fly day" in German). In this contest, people build human-powered flying machines and launch them off a thirty-foot platform. The plane that flies the farthest before crashing into the lake wins.

Red Bull made its way around Europe in the early 1990s and finally came to the United States in 1997. Its success inspired hundreds of copycats, including Jolt, Monster Energy, and Rockstar. In less than five years, more than three hundred brands of energy drinks flooded the US market.

There must be a lot of tired people out there.

Although sports drinks help you rehydrate, so does water. Endurance athletes might benefit from the extra glucose and electrolytes, but most of us don't sweat enough to deplete our reserves. However, sports drinks are perfect for rehydrating after a stomach bug. Diarrhea and vomiting are quick routes to dehydration, and sipping on a sports drink can aid in recovery.

Energy drinks typically have some B vitamins, as well as niacin, calcium, sodium, the amino acids taurine and phenylalanine, and a lot of caffeine. Some brands have as much as 300 milligrams of caffeine per can, which is three times the recommended daily amount for young people between the ages of thirteen and eighteen. Since energy drinks became popular in the late 1990s, there's been a dramatic increase in the number of caffeine overdoses reported in emergency rooms.

TOP IT OFF

- In 2020, 7.9 billion cans of Red Bull were sold across the globe.
- An eighteen-year-old Austrian man, Andreas Mihavecz, survived eighteen days without water in 1979. He had been arrested and put into a holding cell, but the guards forgot about him. He managed to stay alive by licking condensation off the walls of his cell.
- Gatorade was the leading sports drink in the United States in 2020 with sales over 1.6 billion dollars.
- You can die from drinking too much water. Hyponatremia is a potentially fatal condition caused by taking in water faster than the kidneys can process it, causing the sodium levels in the blood to get out of balance.

✳✳ Concoction Corner ✳✳

A perfect postgame treat for hard-playing athletes or little ones recovering from tummy troubles, this citrusy gelatin snack offers more than just a twang for the taste buds; it replaces some of the electrolytes lost in action.

ELECTRIFYING ELECTROLYTE JELLIES

YOU'LL NEED:

- Cooking spray, for pan
- 4 (3-ounce) boxes of orange-flavored gelatin
- 2½ cups of lemon-lime flavored sports drink

Spray a 9-by-13-inch pan with cooking spray.

Heat the sports drink in the pan until just boiling, then remove from the heat. Mix in the boxes of gelatin. Stir for at least 2 to 3 minutes. Pour the mixture into the pan. Chill for 3 to 4 hours. When you are ready to cut into shapes (cookie cutters are fun), dip the bottom of the pan in warm water for a few seconds to loosen the gelatin. For less sugar, use sugar-free gelatin and/or a low-sugar sports drink. Would you prefer less citrus? Pick other fun flavors.

Selected Sources

When I started researching the history of our favorite drinks, I used books, the internet, newspapers, magazines, and experiments. There isn't enough room for all the sources I used, so I selected the most important ones. If you would like to see the complete source list, contact me at KimZachman.com.

CHAPTER ONE
Water, Water, Everywhere . . .

Cartwright, Mark. "Roman Baths." *World History Encyclopedia*. Last updated May 2, 2013. Worldhistory.org/Roman_baths.

Folger, Tim. "The Cuyahoga River Caught Fire 50 Years Ago. It Inspired a Movement." *National Geographic*. June 21, 2019. Nationalgeographic.com/environment/article/the-cuyahoga-river-caught-fire-it-inspired-a-movement.

Gleick, Peter H. *Bottled & Sold: The Story behind Our Obsession with Bottled Water*. Washington , DC: Island Press, 2010.

Hansman, Heather. "A New Efficient Filter Helps Astronauts Drink Their Own Urine." *Smithsonian Magazine*. September 11, 2015. Smithsonianmag.com/innovation/new-efficient-filter-helps-astronauts-drink-their-own-urine-180956499.

"Hot Springs." *World of Phenomena*. Accessed October 18, 2021. Phenomena.org/geological/hotspring.

Robertson, Sally. "Lead Poisoning History." News Medical. Last updated February 26, 2019. News-medical.net/health/lead-poisoning-history.aspx.

Salzman, James. *Drinking Water: A History*. New York: Overlook Duckworth, 2017.

Siegel, Seth M. *Troubled Water: What's Wrong with What We Drink*. New York: Thomas Dunne Books, 2019.

"Water Facts—Worldwide Water Supply." Bureau of Reclamation California-Great Basin. Last updated November 11, 2020. Usbr.gov/mp/arwec/water-facts-ww-water-sup.html.

CHAPTER TWO
Milk It for All It's Worth

Crowley, Carolyn Hughes. "The Man Who Invented Elsie, the Borden Cow." *Smithsonian Magazine*. August 31, 1999. Smithsonianmag.com/science-nature/the-man-who-invented-elsie-the-borden-cow-171931492.

"Definition & Facts for Lactose Intolerance." National Institute of Diabetes and Digestive and Kidney Diseases. Last updated February 2018. Niddk.nih.gov/health-information/digestive-diseases/lactose-intolerance/definition-facts.

"Evolution: It Does a Body Good." *Science.* February 26, 2007. Sciencemag.org/news/2007/02/evolution-it-does-body-good.

Gwinn, David Marshall. "Four Hundred Years of Milk in America." *New York History* 31, no. 4 (October 1950): 448–462.

"Koch's Discovery of the Tubercle Bacillus." Centers for Disease Control and Prevention. March 19, 1982. Cdc.gov/mmwr/preview/mmwrhtml/00000222.htm.

Kurlansky, Mark. *Milk! A 10,000-Year Food Fracas.* New York: Bloomsbury Publishing, 2018.

"Nathan Straus." Jewish Virtual Library. Jewishvirtuallibrary.org/Nathan-straus. Accessed August 21, 2021.

Trout, G. M. "Official Acceptance of Homogenized Milk in the United States." *Journal of Dairy Science* 46, no. 4 (April 1963): 342–345. doi.org/10.3168/jds.S0022-0302(63)89045-1. Accessed August 27, 2021.

CHAPTER THREE
All the Tea in China

Begley, Sarah. "A Brief History of the Tea Bag." *Time.* September 3, 2015. Time.com/3996712/a-brief-history-of-the-tea-bag.

Heiss, Mary Lou, and Robert J. Heiss. *The Story of Tea: A Cultural History and Drinking Guide.* Berkeley, CA: Ten Speed Press, 2007.

Koehler, Jeff. "How Lipton Built an Empire by Selling 'Farm to Table' Tea." The Salt, NPR. October 25, 2016. Npr.org/sections/thesalt/2016/10/25/498863411/-from-tea-garden-to-teapot-how-lipton-became-an-empire.

MacFarlane, Alan, and Iris MacFarlane. *The Empire of Tea: The Remarkable History of the Plant That Took Over the World.* New York: The Overlook Press, 2004.

McHugh, Tara. "How Tea Is Processed." *Food Technology Magazine.* January 1, 2018. Ift.org/news-and-publications/food-technology-magazine/issues/2018/January/columns/processing-how-tea-is-processed.

Reader's Digest Association. *Food Cures: Heal What Ails You with Delicious Superfoods!* White Plains, NY: Reader's Digest Books, 2019.

Standage, Tom. *A History of the World in 6 Glasses.* New York: Bloomsbury, 2005.

Tea Association of the U.S.A., Inc. "Tea Fact Sheet—2022." TeaUSA.com/teausa/images/Tea-Fact-2021.pdf. Accessed October 2, 2021.

CHAPTER FOUR
Wake Up!

Clark, Taylor. *Starbucked: A Double Tall Tale of Caffeine, Commerce, and Culture.* New York: Little, Brown and Company, 2007.

Funderburg, Anne Cooper. "Cowboy Coffee." *True West.* July 1, 2001. Truewestmagazine.com/cowboy-coffee.

McGinn, Daniel. "The Inside Story of Keurig's Rise to a Billion-Dollar Coffee Empire." *The Boston Globe.* August 7, 2011. Archive.boston.com/business/articles/2011/08/07/the_inside_story_of_keurigs_rise_to_a_billion_dollar_coffee_empire.

Pendergrast, Mark. *Uncommon Grounds: The History of Coffee and How It Transformed Our World.* New York: Basic Books, 2019.

Smith, Andrew F. *Drinking History: Fifteen Turning Points in the Making of American Beverages.* New York: Columbia University Press, 2012.

Stewart, Amy. *The Drunken Botanist: The Plants That Create the World's Great Drinks.* Chapel Hill, NC: Algonquin Books, 2013.

US Department of Agriculture and US Department of Health and Human Services. *Dietary Guidelines for Americans, 2020–2025.* 9th ed. December 2020. DietaryGuidelines.gov.

Uusilehto, Jenni. "What Is Coffee Cupping?" Barista Institute. Baristainstitute.com/inspiration/what-coffee-cupping. Accessed September 9, 2021.

CHAPTER FIVE
There's No Cream in Cream Soda

Calandro, Daniel. "Hudson River Valley Icehouses and Ice Industry." Hudson River Valley Institute Student Works. May 9, 2005. hudsonrivervalley.org/documents/401021/1058093/NatIceIndustrydicehousepaper.pdf/0d886800-535e-4fdb-8afc-ae7b0e751661.

Funderburg, Anne Cooper. *Sundae Best: A History of Soda Fountains.* Bowling Green, OH: Bowling Green State University Press, 2002.

"Joseph Priestley (1733–1804)." Science History Institute. Last updated December 14, 2017. Sciencehistory.org/historical-profile/joseph-priestley.

Nosowitz, Dan. "Why Is Cream Soda Called 'Cream' Anyway?" *Bon Appétit.* March 9, 2017. Bonappetit.com/story/cream-soda-history.

Ostrow, Lonnie. "L'chaim to Dr. Brown, Most Enduring Kosher Soft Drink." *The Jewish Star.* August 18, 2014. Thejewishstar.com/stories/lchaim-to-dr-brown-most-enduring-kosher-soft-drink,5219.

Smith, Andrew F. *Drinking History: Fifteen Turning Points in the Making of American Beverages.* New York: Columbia University Press, 2012.

Young-Witzel, Gyvel, and Michael Karl Witzel. *Soda Pop! From Miracle Medicine to Pop Culture.* Stillwater, MN: Town Square Books, 1998.

CHAPTER SIX
At the Root of It

Chase, Alvin Wood. *Dr. Chase's Recipes: or, Information for Everybody: An Invaluable Collection of About Eight Hundred Practical Recipes.* United States: R. A. Beal, 1870.

Coffey, R. Kelley. "Sassafras in America." *The Appalachian Voice.* November 1, 2003. Appvoices.org/2003/11/01/2780.

Hingston, Sandy. "10 Things You Might Not Know about Root Beer Magnate Charles Hires." City Life, *Philadelphia Magazine.* June 5, 2018. Phillymag.com/2018/06/05/hires-root -beer-book.

"James Cook Ayer, Sarsaparilla King of Lowell, Mass." New England Historical Society. Last updated in 2022. Newenglandhistoricalsociety.com/james-cook-ayer-sarsaparilla -king-lowell-mass.

Reader's Digest Association. *Food Cures: Heal What Ails You with Delicious Superfoods!* New York: Reader's Digest Books, 2019.

Smith, Andrew F. *Drinking History: Fifteen Turning Points in the Making of American Beverages.* New York: Columbia University Press, 2012.

Stewart, Amy. *The Drunken Botanist: The Plants That Create the World's Great Drinks.* Chapel Hill, NC: Algonquin Books, 2013.

Young-Witzel, Gyvel, and Michael Karl Witzel. *Soda Pop! From Miracle Medicine to Pop Culture.* Stillwater, MN: Town Square Books, 1998.

CHAPTER SEVEN
Cola Wars

Irwin, Sam. "Sugar Policy Ensures Adequate Supplies in a Crisis." American Sugar Cane League. May 4, 2020. Amscl.org/sugar-policy-ensures-adequate-supplies-in-a-crisis.

Neuman, Scott. "Aluminum's Strange Journey from Precious Metal to Beer Can." Short Wave, NPR. December 10, 2019. Npr.org/2019/12/05/785099705/aluminums-strange-journey -from-precious-metal-to-beer-can.

Pendergrast, Mark. *For God, Country & Coca-Cola: The Definitive History of the Great American Soft Drink and the Company That Makes It,* 3rd ed. New York: Basic Books, 2013.

Stewart, Amy. *The Drunken Botanist: The Plants That Create the World's Great Drinks*. Chapel Hill, NC: Algonquin Books, 2013.

"A Time for Innovation." Can Manufacturers Institute. Cancentral.com/can-stats/history-of-the-can/time-innovation. Accessed February 12, 2022.

Young-Witzel, Gyvel, and Michael Karl Witzel. *Soda Pop! From Miracle Medicine to Pop Culture*. Stillwater, MN: Town Square Books, 1998.

CHAPTER EIGHT
Squeezed!

"Advertising Brought Grape Juice to Fame." *The Indianapolis Star*. April 17, 1915.

Aguilar, Jen. "The Marvelous History of Lemonade." *Herald Weekly*. February 17, 2022. Heraldweekly.com/the-marvelous-history-of-lemonade.

"Albert Szent-Györgyi's Discovery of Vitamin C." American Chemical Society National Historic Chemical Landmarks. Acs.org/content/acs/en/education/whatischemistry/landmarks/szentgyorgyi.html. Accessed March 2, 2022.

Danovich, Tove. "How Lemonade Helped Paris Fend Off Plague and Other Surprising 'Food Fights.'" The Salt, NPR. March 12, 2017. Npr.org/thesalt/2017/03/12/519460915/how-lemonade-helped-paris-fend-off-plague-and-other-surprising-food-fights.

Gollner, Adam Leith. *The Fruit Hunters: A Story of Nature, Adventure, Commerce, and Obsession*. New York: Scribner, 2008.

Hamilton, Alissa. *Squeezed: What You Don't Know about Orange Juice*. New Haven, CT: Yale University Press, 2009.

Kiniry, Laura. "The Unusual Origins of Pink Lemonade." *Smithsonian Magazine*. August 16, 2016. Smithsonianmag.com/history/unusual-origins-pink-lemonade-180960145.

Merlo, Catherine. *Heritage of Gold: The First 100 Years of Sunkist Growers, Inc. 1893–1993*. Sunkist Growers, Inc., 1993.

Pucci, Dan, and Craig Cavallo. *American Cider: A Modern Guide to a Historic Beverage*. New York: Ballentine Books, 2021.

CHAPTER NINE
Packets and Pouches of Punches

Barber, Casey. "Tang! The Space-Age Drink That's Still a Worldwide Staple." CNN. Last updated May 1, 2021. Cnn.com/2021/05/01/world/tang-space-age-scn-wellness/index.html.

Barrows, Julie N., Arthur L. Lipman, and Catherine J. Bailey. "Color Additives History." *Food Safety Magazine*. October/November 2003. Fda.gov/industry/color-additives/color-additives-history.

Blutz, Matt. "How NASA Made Tang Cool." *Food and Wine.* May 18, 2017. Foodandwine.com/lifestyle/how-nasa-made-tang-cool.

"Dunedin Plant Plays Part in Foster's Success Story." *Tampa Bay Times.* October 15, 1953.

Gibbens, Sarah. "A Brief History of How Plastic Straws Took Over the World." *National Geographic.* January 2, 2019. Nationalgeographic.com/environment/article/news-plastic-drinking-straw-history-ban.

Kreutzer-Hodson, Teresa. "Kool-Aid." History Nebraska. History.nebraska.gov/publications/kool-aid. Accessed September 17, 2021.

Lazarus, George. "Capri Sun Blazing in the Fruit Drink Market." *Chicago Tribune.* June 3, 1982.

"The Refreshing History of Punch Bowls." *Southern Home.* November 18, 2021. Southernhomemagazine.com/2021/11/18/refreshing-history-punch-bowls.

Rohrig, Brian. "Eating with Your Eyes: The Chemistry of Food Colorings." American Chemical Society. October 2015. Acs.org/content/acs/en/education/resources/highschool/chemmatters/past-issues/2015-2016/october-2015/food colorings.html.

Smith, Andrew F. *Drinking History: Fifteen Turning Points in the Making of American Beverages.* New York: Columbia University Press, 2012.

"Zoo's Twiga Will Have 2 Giraffe Friends Soon." *Honolulu Star-Bulletin.* September 24, 1956.

CHAPTER TEN
Game On!

Abbott, Karen. "The 1904 Olympic Marathon May Have Been the Strangest Ever." *Smithsonian Magazine.* August 7, 2012. Smithsonianmag.com/history/the-1904-Olympic-marathon-may-have-been-the-strangest-ever-14910747.

Amdur, Neil. "Florida's Pause That Refreshes: Nip of 'Gatorade.'" *Miami Herald.* November 30, 1966.

Aschwanden, Christie. *Good to Go: What the Athlete in All of Us Can Learn from the Strange Science of Recovery.* New York: W. W. Norton & Company, 2019.

Magness, Steve. "The History of Hydration: A Lesson in the Scientific Method and the Hype Cycle." *Science of Running.* January 1, 2011. Scienceofrunning.com/2011/01/history-of-hydration-lesson-in.html?v=47e5dceea252.

Nix, Elizabeth. "Why Is a Marathon 26.2 Miles?" History. Updated August 2, 2021. History.com/news/why-is-a-marathon-26-2-miles.

Rovell, Darren. *First in Thirst: How Gatorade Turned the Science of Sweat into a Cultural Phenomenon.* New York: Amacom, 2006.

Smith, Andrew F. *Drinking History: Fifteen Turning Points in the Making of American Beverages.* New York: Columbia University Press, 2012.

Acknowledgments

When I found out that I'd get to work with editor Allison Cohen again, I popped open a bottle to celebrate . . . a bottle of cream soda, of course. Allison's vision for *There's No Ham in Hamburgers* exceeded my expectations, and I couldn't wait to see what she would do with *There's No Cream in Cream Soda*. Working with the whole Running Press Kids team has been a delight. Thanks to our book designer, Frances Soo Ping Chow; production editor, Melanie Gold; marketing and publicity team, Becca Matheson and Kara Thornton; copy editor, Shasta Clinch; and proofreader, Lori Paximadis. And I'm so thankful to have the wonderfully talented Peter Donnelly illustrating again.

Of course, none of this would've happened if my agent, John Rudolph, hadn't taken a chance on me. Thanks, John!

Writing is a solitary craft, but fortunately for me, not a lonely one. I'm honored to be a member of an excellent critique group. Thank you, Kristine Anderson, Lela Bridgers, Debbie D'Aurelio, Sherry Ellis, Danny Schnitzlein, and Lisa Lewis Tyre, for all your suggestions. I also want to thank Lisa Maguire for some last-minute proofreading and Nora McFarland for the pick-me-ups when I needed them.

My mom, Rita Hackler, has always been my biggest cheerleader, and her confidence in me lifted my spirits when self-doubt was dragging me down.

Thanks to my children, Aspen and Josie, for patiently listening to me talk about the book. They bravely asked me how it was going, even though they knew they would get an earful.

There's no way I could have my dream job as a children's author if it wasn't for the support of my husband, Dan. He's been there for me in the little ways and the big ways and not just while I was writing this book.

I raise my glass in a toast to you all!

Index

When **KIM ZACHMAN** was a kid, she drove her parents crazy asking questions. She still asks lots of questions, and when she finds fun, fascinating answers, she writes about them. Kim lives in Roswell, Georgia, with her husband and their almost perfect dog.

PETER DONNELLY is an award-winning illustrator who is influenced by midcentury design, folk art, and vintage print. He lives and works in Ireland.

Inventions and Innovations in Beverage History

~2450 BCE—Shen-Nung discovers tea. (China)

206 BCE–220 BCE—Chinese porcelain was invented during the Han dynasty. (China)

700–800 CE—Coffee is discovered. (Ethiopia)

1759—Wedgwood pottery business is founded by Josiah Wedgwood. (England)

1772—Joseph Priestley develops method to carbonate water. (England)

1783—First mass-produced carbonated water by Jacob Schweppe. (Switzerland)

1809—Soda fountain invented by Joseph Hawkins. (Philadelphia, Pennsylvania)

1854—Dr. John Snow uses the "Ghost Map" to track a cholera outbreak. (London, England)

1856—Borden's canned Sweetened Condensed Milk produced and sold. (Wolcottville, Connecticut)

1865—Louis Pasteur develops pasteurization. (France)

1866—Vernor's Ginger Ale created by James Vernor. (Detroit, Michigan)

1869—Thomas Welch develops Welch's Grape Juice. (Vineland, New Jersey)

1876—Charles E. Hires develops instant root beer. (Philadelphia, Pennsylvania)

1879—Hutchinson's stopper for glass bottles is patented by Charles G. Hutchinson. (Chicago, Illinois)

1882—Robert Koch identifies the bacteria that causes tuberculosis. (Germany)

1884—Sealable milk bottle "The Milk Protector" invented by Dr. Henry G. Thatcher. (Potsdam, New York)

1885—Dr Pepper is created by Charles Alderton. (Waco, Texas)

1886—Dr. Brown's cream soda is bottled and sold. (New York, New York)

1886—Coca-Cola is developed by John Pemberton. (Atlanta, Georgia)

1888—Paper straw invented by Marvin Stone. (Washington, D. C.)

1892—Crown bottle caps are invented by William Painter. (Baltimore, Maryland.)

1894—Pepsi-Cola is created by Caleb Bradham. (New Bern, North Carolina)

1901—Roberta Lawson and Mary Molaren invent the tea bag. (Milwaukee, Wisconsin)

1904—Automated glass bottle machine developed by Michael Owens. (Toledo, Ohio)